HOW TO MAKE A

Wildlife Garden

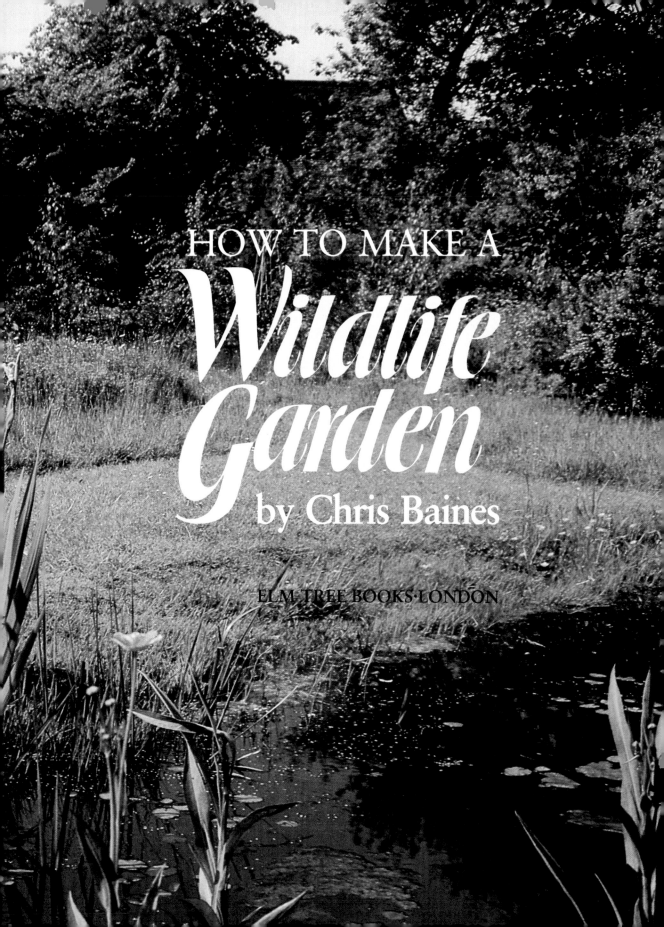

HOW TO MAKE A
Wildlife Garden

by Chris Baines

ELM TREE BOOKS·LONDON

First published in Great Britain 1985
by Elm Tree Books/Hamish Hamilton Ltd
Garden House 57–59 Long Acre London WC2E 9JZ

Copyright © 1985 by J. Christopher Baines
Book design by Norman Reynolds

Drawings by Jim Bridgen

British Library Cataloguing in Publication Data

Baines, Chris
    How to make a wildlife garden.
    1.Wildlife habitat improvement   2.Garden
    ecology
    I.Title
    639.9'2   SK355

    ISBN 0-241-11448-9

Filmset by MS Filmsetting Limited, Frome
Printed and bound in Spain
by Cayfosa Industria Gráfica, Barcelona

    Dep. leg. B-4525-1985

Contents

All photographs by Chris Baines except kestrel (p. III), fox (p. 163) by Mike Leach/Saxon photographic; dragonfly (p. 83), hoverfly (p. 130), moths (pp. 175 & 179), hedgehog (p. 167) by Tony Wharton; nestbox (p. 143) by G. W. Ward/Aquila Photographics; woodpecker (p.162) by Eric Hosking; Dutch nursery (p. 114–5) by Rob Leopold

PART 1
Why make a Wildlife Garden?

ABOVE: **Be brave!** Leave your weedy old lawn uncut for a week or two in June or July and you may be surprised to find all kinds of beautiful little wild flowers appearing.

Chapter 1

Why wildlife?

MOST PEOPLE have an instinctive love of nature. You can see it in the way children rush to feed the ducks in the park. You can feel it in the thrill of seeing an urban fox streaking through the beam of your car's headlights. When a butterfly is trapped in the house, you automatically open a window and carefully guide it back to freedom.

Getting 'back to nature' seems to be essential if we are to cope with the strains of modern life. Just a few minutes of quiet relaxation amongst trees, with bird song and bumblebees for entertainment, and even the most exhausted of city workers is ready for anything. Certainly a quiet five minutes stroll through my garden first thing in the morning, with dew still wet on the grass, and a bowl of cornflakes in my hand, seems to make the perfect start to a working day. There is something magical, too, about the feeling that you are sharing your landscape with a whole host of wild creatures. Some are obvious. Town blackbirds will hop just a safe few feet ahead of you, stopping every now and then for a sideways glance in your direction, and a quick jab at some poor unfortunate snack. Many of the larger creatures, particularly the mammals, avoid confrontation by operating under cover of darkness. Take the trouble to join them in the late evening twilight, and a minute or two of silent waiting will be rewarded with the snuffles, scuffles and grunts of hedgehogs, field mice and the various other night visitors that share your landscape.

In most green spaces there is a pretty healthy community of this sort of Big Game – the cuddly creatures, the fluffy feathered friends, the wildlife you can spot at fifty yards. It's fascinating to watch, and comforting to have around. For most people, though, the variety of large animals and birds they are likely to see on their doorstep is fairly limited. The real excitement, the really amazing variety of wildlife lives in the scaled-down world of tangled grasses, bramble leaves and rotting logs. Choose a leafy spot, sit quietly for five minutes and watch this mini-jungle carefully. As your eyes become accustomed to the new scale you will gradually begin to see more and more amazing creatures, all making a secret living right under your nose. If you want to spend a really exciting and totally absorbing half hour 'on safari' sometime, just take a metre or so of string and a magnifying glass. Run the string through a patch of mini-jungle, get down on your hands and knees, and work your way slowly along your portable nature-trail.

Needless to say, all of this 'nature' is important for much more than its entertainment value. It's not too fanciful to suppose that an environment which is healthy for mini-beasts is also healthy for us – and of course a landscape which is hostile to wildlife must be an unhealthy place for humans to live in. It is frightening, therefore, to discover just *how* hostile we have made our environment in recent times. In two generations we have devastated the natural world with chemical pollution, urban expansion, land drainage, road construction and industrialised agriculture. In my lifetime we have left behind a relatively rich landscape, where cowslips and primroses were common-place, woodland was within walking distance for most people, and butterflies were still part of the standard entertainment on sunny summer days. Those times are just a fond memory now, and 'nature' has been locked away for safe keeping in green museums that we call nature reserves. So far as the preservation of individual species is concerned, that policy might work tolerably well. Put a fence around a bluebell wood, and so long as you continue to manage it positively, cutting the coppice hazel regularly every few years, and controlling the amount of browsing that goes on, there should be bluebells to visit indefinitely. Unfortunately, not all wildlife is as obliging as the bluebell. Dragonflies which breed in nature reserve ponds have a dangerous habit of flying over the fence to hunt their insect prey. All too often the midges on the other side have been 'got at' by some chemical or another, the dragonfly snaps up a few hundred each day, and by the end of the summer, that's one more spectacular insect that fails to make it back to base. British species of dragonfly have become extinct at an alarming rate since the war.

The otter is a more celebrated example of a species which has become almost extinct despite the growth in the number of nature reserves. Otters need large territories. Specifically, they need long stretches of unpolluted stream and river, with banks well wooded. Sadly that combination is almost non-existent in the modern farming countryside. Add to that the requirement for individual territories to connect together if cubs from different families are to meet and interbreed, and you can see why there are so few otters left.

In the past forty years, despite our great national love of nature, we have destroyed 95% of our wildflower meadows, 50% of our ancient lowland woods, 60% of our lowland heaths, 80% of our downland

TOP: Habitat destruction in the Third World is disastrous. An area of tropical rain forest the size of Wales is being destroyed each year in the Amazon Basin – much of it is replaced by short-life cattle grazing to supply cheap hamburgers to the USA. But . . .

BOTTOM: . . . on our own cosy doorstep the conservation record is just as bad. We have destroyed more of this kind of irreplaceable ancient woodland in the past 40 years, than our ancestors managed to wipe out in the previous 400.

OPPOSITE, TOP: Intensive farming is by no means the only agent of destruction. This lovely 50 acre working farm lay in the heart of the industrial Black Country.

OPPOSITE, BOTTOM: In 1982 the powerful property development lobby persuaded central government to declare Merry Hill Farm an Enterprise Zone, and its greenfields and hedgerows were destroyed forever.

sheepwalks, and 50% of our lowland fens and mires. Even now, with so little left, we are destroying the very special places, the Sites of Special Scientific Interest, at a rate of 10% every year. Many of these precious habitats are special because they are ancient and can never be replaced. To grub out an eight thousand-year-old bluebell wood, just to build a new industrial estate, or grow a few more tons of wheat to add to the surplus mountain is as stupid as demolishing Canterbury Cathedral or Stonehenge to build a multi-storey car park, and yet that is exactly what we are doing. We owe it to the rest of the world to provide a suitable home for the nightingales which travel here from Africa to breed each summer. We owe it to our own grandchildren, and their grandchildren, too, to make sure they can still choose to enjoy the fabulous, spine-tingling *sound* of nightingales singing on balmy summer nights.

So what can we do about it? How *can* we reverse the trend, and provide future generations with more wildlife rather than less? Well, first of all we must continue to cling on desperately to those fragments of rich, ancient habitat that still survive. All of them need managing, of course – we have very little, if any, true wilderness in Britain. Where it happens to be traditional farming practice which has produced the habitats, as is the case with water-meadows, cornfield wildflowers and hayfields, then we need to find ways of persuading farmers to continue to manage them along traditional, sensitive but sometimes less productive lines. We need to weight much more heavily the irreplaceable nature of many of these landscapes, when considering such short-life uses as 'science parks', quarries and housing estates. A new warehouse with an economic life expectancy of twenty to thirty years should never be allowed to replace a precious, green wildlife habitat with a life expectancy of – forever!

Many of us tend to feel that as individuals we are powerless – that 'they' will decide. I'm glad to say that, in my experience at least, that certainly isn't so! You can have enormous influence simply by writing a positive letter to the right decision-maker at the right time, since all too often councillors and others are forced to make decisions with only one side of the argument presented to them. Perhaps the most important thing you can do, though, is lend your support to your local environmental group. Throughout Britain there are County Naturalists Trusts for Nature Conservation. You can find out the address of your local County Trust by contacting The Royal Society for Nature Conservation (RSNC), whose address is at the back of the book. At one time they were concerned with nature reserves, species counts and very little else, but most of them are now powerful campaigning organisations too, consulted by local authorities when planning decisions have to be made, and working hard to provide more and better places for wildlife. If you aren't a member of your County Trust already, then you certainly should be. They need your support, and in return you can rely on them to help you fight your battles on behalf of the local wildlife.

The picture I have painted so far is pretty gloomy – a desperately urgent need to cling on to the few remaining fragments of our once-rich natural heritage. So far as the ancient habitats in our farming countryside are concerned, I'm afraid that is absolutely true. Most of the rural landscape is a hostile green desert for wildlife, and ancient meadows, bogs and woodlands cannot be recreated, no matter how much field-corner tree-planting farmers do. There is, however, a silver lining to this big black cloud.

In our villages, towns and cities there is a vast amount of land which no one expects to be highly productive. The average metropolitan conurbation seems at first glance to be a pretty hostile concrete jungle. Noisy traffic, polluting chimneys and sterile tarmac dominate the scene. In fact, the view from the street is very misleading. Climb to the top of a tall building anywhere, in Manchester, Merseyside, Tyneside, Glasgow, Birmingham and you will see what I mean. In fact, even the most congested of towns and cities is more green than black. And the green space in towns is all available for nature conservation – no milk quota to satisfy here! The urban area I am most familiar with is the West Midlands, but I know from my childhood in Sheffield that the story in South Yorkshire is much the same. Certainly the main roads are flanked by cliffs of hostile buildings, though the pigeons and starlings seem to make very good use of the poor insulation and the free heating that leaks out each night, since they choose to roost there in vast numbers. Behind these concrete canyons, though, the West Midlands is a fantastic tapestry of green. The railway lines, canals, road verges and river valleys provide a continuous network of rich, green ecological corridors – ideal for wildlife to move along. Most people are familiar with the kestrels that hunt for small mammals and large insects along the verges of the urban clearways. Many people have seen the foxes that clear up the debris of chip papers and dropped ice creams in the city centre after the last bus has left, and we know that they travel in from the leafy suburbs along the commuter railway lines. Kingfishers have followed the canals, and now nest deep in the heart of England's second city, presumably enjoying the sticklebacks which live in the unpolluted water, and undoubtedly benefiting from the slightly warmer winter temperatures which mean less ice to cope with. There are definite advantages to town life for a great many of our wild creatures.

The corridor system is vitally important if wildlife is to move around. Certainly there is plenty of evidence of a move into the towns for the more spectacular large predators – foxes, stoats, hedgehogs, kestrels, herons, even badgers are beginning to find rural life too much of a strain and are lumbering along the railway cutting to pastures new among the shrubberies and overgrown tennis courts of Victorian suburban gardens.

OVERLEAF: Intensive chemical agriculture has squeezed out almost all the wildlife from our farming countryside. This may be highly *productive*, but it is also extremely *inefficient* in its use of non-renewable energy resources. It degrades the soil, and has done irreparable harm to our natural heritage.

These corridors are equally important for the less dramatic wildlife. This is obvious if you think about it, since the predators are only there for the rich pickings provided by the smaller creatures, and they, in turn, all depend directly or indirectly on the availability of a rich diversity of plant life. Stand by a railway line in late August and you will see how successfully the clouds of rosebay willow herb and thistle seed manage to hitch a lift in the slip-stream of the 9.47. The birds and animals that move along the corridor will inevitably transport the sticky, hooked fruit of species such as burdock (sticky willie) and goosegrass (cleavers) a little further into town – just take a look at your socks and trousers after five minutes of jungle-bashing. Many plants are very good at moving around. You can plot the progress of large plants quite easily, particularly where a new corridor is created – say for example on the embankments of the latest section of the ring road. Provided the soil isn't too rich, and the gangmowers are kept at bay, you will see saplings of the trees and shrubs with windborne seed spring up almost immediately. Silver birch and goat willow are the classic first colonisers, birch having a very very light, flat seed-case, and goat willow floating along with a little cotton wool cloud in much the same style as a dandelion parachute. You may also have the winged seed of ash and sycamore spinning in and germinating. Within five or six years the front line of pioneer birch and willow will themselves be mature enough to produce seed of their own, and so blow on for another few hundred metres.

Once the pioneers have produced a branch or two, birds will roost there. Inevitably the fruit-eaters, such as blackbirds and thrushes, will leave behind a sprinkling of hawthorn, elder, rose and other shrub seeds – all conveniently stripped of their juicy outer fruit and specially prepared for instant germination. Within a year or two the birch will be surrounded by a thicket of bramble, wild-briar and May-blossom. A year or two later, this scrub will be generating blackberries and rosehips of its own, to feed the birds that carry the seed further along the corridor.

Of course the green corridors are only a part of the wildlife resource in towns, but they have the advantage of being easy to identify and now, at last, local planning authorities are beginning to adopt official policies of protection for the ecological network. The West Midlands Metropolitan County Council, for example, now has a strategy plan for nature conservation.

Go up to the top of your tower block, or look at an aerial photograph of the neighbourhood, and you will see that the corridors link together a great number of 'green bulges'. Sometimes the bulge may be no bigger than a traffic island or a quarter acre building plot, but there are huge bulges too. There are the unofficial landscapes: the quarries, railway sidings, overgrown demolition sites and abandoned sewage works; and there are the official green spaces: the parks and the playing fields around schools and colleges. Together all of this land adds up to a vast area, hundreds of thousands of acres of land which has no need to be sprayed with chemicals. Land which should be used as creatively as possible, to make up for the loss of wildlife habitat in the countryside. Urban greenspace has the added advantage that almost nine-tenths of our population live in towns and so the wildlife of the canal, the quarry, the refuse tip and the public park is accessible and familiar.

Generally speaking, the unofficial wasteland sites are much richer in wildlife than the official public open spaces. Derelict wasteland is particularly good for coarse weed species such as thistles, docks and teasels, and these attract clouds of butterflies in the summer and large flocks of seed-eating finches in the winter. There is quite often a drainage problem on wasteland sites. Water collects in compacted hollows, or fills up old basements, and permanent pools are quickly adopted as breeding habitat for amphibians and aquatic insects, whilst the temporary winter wetlands provide a very important resting point for the migrant ducks, geese and waders that fly to Britain from the frozen north each year.

By contrast, the public parks and playing fields are very neat and tidy, and the traditional landscape of close-mown grass and parkland trees is a relatively poor habitat for wildlife. It does have tremendous capabilities though. Some of the parkland grass is full of wildflowers, chopped off by the mower blades week after week. A number of the trees are very old indeed, perhaps dating back to a time long before Victorian parks, when the local landscape was woods and fields. The parks offer tremendous potential for habitat creation. A change in the mowing pattern can produce wildflower meadows almost instantly. An underplanting of hazel, holly, foxgloves and primroses can turn the lonely specimen trees into the top canopy of a rich new woodland within a season or two. There is scope for converting redundant boating lakes to marsh and reed-bed, flooding the badly drained sports pitch to provide wildfowl habitat, and generally 'roughing the place up a bit' in the interest of wildlife. Many people would find more reason to visit the park if there were more birds and butterflies around, if the grassland was sprinkled with cowslips in the spring, and if there were brambles and hazelnuts to harvest in the autumn. If that kind of park appeals to you, tell your local authority. There is plenty of scope for creative conservation as well as formal sports provision. If even 10% of the close mown grass was allowed to flower and was cut for hay, then we would very soon hear skylarks in our cities, and there would be far more butterflies around for town-dwellers to enjoy. When you apply the same ideas to school grounds, hospital landscapes, airports, power stations and all the other official green landscapes we pay people to manage, then you can see what tremendous scope there is for helping wildlife, and making our life in towns more colourful and interesting.

Children are leading the way with conservation. This group of city kids is caring for a mini-woodland they helped plant a year earlier on demolition rubble close to their homes, in the middle of Walsall. No vandalism, no dead trees and lots of fun.

Of course a very major part of the green space in villages, towns and cities is provided by private gardens. Your garden or mine may seem small and insignificant on its own, but when you add all the garden space together it covers a huge area, and very often a row of leafy gardens can provide a vital wildlife corridor link in itself. Gardens are relatively quiet, generally sheltered, and they often follow the line of much older landscape features. If you have a hawthorn hedge, a line of trees or a ditch running along the back edge of your garden, then the odds are that it is a relic of the rural landscape that existed before the houses were built. That may mean it dates back hundreds of years, and therefore the habitat will have the added bonus of a long history, in which the wildlife will have had the chance to build up into a quite complex community.

If you adopt the accepted practices of twentieth century gardening, then you will be planting exotic shrubs and flowers, and generally putting the local wildlife under exactly the same kind of hostile pressure that has done so much harm in the farming countryside. Adopt a more sensitive approach. See how many things you can persuade to *live* in your garden, instead of notching up more and more things to kill. Even the smallest of town gardens can provide a rich and valuable sanctuary for a whole host of wildlife. Nobble your neighbours. Persuade them to plant a hedge, use less pesticide, dig a pond or simply stop burning the autumn leaves, and in no time at all you'll notice the increase of bird life, the boost in the number of butterflies, and your garden will start to look, smell and sound different. You will have a garden with life in it, and you will be playing a part in the whole business of saving a safe place for nature.

Chapter 2

A special role for gardens

THERE ARE a million acres of private gardens in Britain, and the area is increasing, particularly in the inner city, as the high-rise horror tower-blocks of the '60s are being replaced by more traditional new houses with gardens. The County Naturalist Trusts manage a total of about 100,000 acres of nature reserves between them, so you can see that in area alone, private gardens represent a land source which is worth taking seriously.

As I have already suggested, we can't hope to solve the whole nature conservation problem with domestic gardens. Wildlife gardens will never provide a habitat for the osprey, the red deer or the otter, but they can make an enormous difference to the well-being of a huge variety of plants and animals. Much of Britain used to be covered with deciduous woodland before man began clearing the land for farming. There would be the occasional glade where a large tree had collapsed, or wild deer had cropped the tree seedlings, and along the stream and river courses there would be patches of disturbed ground. Collapsed river cliffs and shingle beaches would have provided habitat for the colourful wildflowers which rapidly moved in and were labelled 'weeds of cultivation' when man began digging the soil. These 'weeds' became the cornfield wild-flowers – poppies, cornflowers, corn-marigolds, corncockle – and agriculture kept them common until the chemical revolution made it possible for farmers to cultivate the soil and kill the seedling wildflowers at the same time. Since woodland was the major habitat in Britain for so long, many of our native plants and animals are most at home in the dappled shade of the woodland edge, or on disturbed ground. These are the two basic types of habitat which the average garden offers, and that is why garden birds such as the blackbird and the dunnock are so obviously at home. They scratch around amongst the fallen leaves of your shrub bed in just the same way as their ancestors must have done amongst the leaf-litter of the primeval forest.

This woodland glade environment is our own natural primitive habitat too. We feel comfortably protected in a sheltered leafy glade, so a garden that suits us as a place to live in is bound to suit a great many of our favourite wild plants and animals.

Left to its own devices, nature has a great ability to settle into a balanced state. The natural woodland plant communities develop on several layers, with each canopy soaking up a little more of the light until the woodland wildflowers at carpet level have just enough sunshine to flower in early spring, before the upper canopies come into leaf. In a similarly balanced way, there will be just enough predators around to eat up most of the plant-eating creepy crawlies, and so prevent them from destroying the habitat itself. By gardening, we automatically disturb that balance in many ways, and I think the secret of a successful wildlife garden depends on understanding the way in which your various gardening activities will distort the balance. The greater the diversity of wildlife, the more enjoyment you will have, but a good deal of orthodox modern gardening practice disturbs the balance in a very negative way, and reduces the variety of wildlife able to survive.

'Live and let live' should be the maxim. Think long and hard before you kill anything, or tidy anything away – and if that sounds like an open invitation to *relax* in the garden, then you're getting the message.

There are lots of ways in which you can give your garden the woodland edge structure talked of earlier, but the real key to rich wildlife depends on the way you *manage* your patch. First of all, minimise disturbance. If your planting develops as a series of layers, with plants tightly packed together, there will be no spare light filtering through to stimulate 'weeds' to grow, and no need for you to crash around in the undergrowth pulling them out. The more timid wild creatures – the hedgehogs, dunnocks and wrens, will be able to move around unmolested.

A rich wildlife garden will be particularly good for insects – you really will notice how many more hoverflies, bumblebees and ladybirds there are around. These too form a balanced community, and modern chemical gardening can play havoc with the inter-relationship between 'pests' and predators. When the aphids appear in the spring, and start sucking the sap from your prize broad beans, it is very tempting to whack them with the latest chemical spray. Look very carefully before you take the plunge. Within days of the blackfly appearing, you will find strange, wrinkled grey maggots wriggling along the same stems wiping out hundreds of blackfly with the efficiency of tiny vacuum cleaners. These are the larvae of ladybirds, and the familiar adults are just as efficient at snapping up aphids. Spray the pest, and you will almost certainly kill the natural predator. What is more, the pest, in this case the blackfly, is able to return and multiply far more quickly than the predator, the ladybird, so hey presto, with one squirt of your aerosol killer spray you have set up the next generation of aphids with a predator-free life of luxury, and goodness knows what special ingredients you've added to your future Sunday lunch.

The really exciting thing about gardening for wildlife, is that you can begin to distort the balance in *favour* of wildlife. Your semi-detached woodland glade can provide a richer, safer habitat than any that ever existed in nature, because you can boost the habitat. You are probably doing that already. Your flower borders provide a surplus of nectar and pollen which brings butterflies and bees from miles around. The peanuts on your bird table help keep dozens of local bluetits alive through the long, hard winter and you may well have a nest box or two, providing a safe alternative nesting site for the small birds that would more naturally choose to build in a hollow log or a rotting branch. In the next few chapters I will show you how you can improve the rich habitats in your garden, or create them from scratch if you are just starting, so that a wide variety of plants and animals will move in permanently, but it is also important to realise the potential there is for habitat extras. The winter bird food, the banks of perfumed flowers, the bowl of drinking water, these will all help to improve your garden as a 'service station' for passing wildlife – wild animals which need a bigger territory than you can provide, or some special habitat feature such as a dead tree or a flowing stream which you simply can't fit into your garden – but which drop into your wildlife garden for an extra snack. Some of these service-station visitors may travel a very long way, too. In summer, you could have painted-lady butterflies from North Africa and garden warblers from south of the Sahara. In the winter months you will almost certainly have starlings from Scandinavia squabbling over the scraps, you may have Swedish siskins on your bag of peanuts, and redwings and fieldfares from as far away as Northern Russia. Exciting, isn't it, to think that your little wildlife garden can actually be making a significant contribution to international nature conservation!

There is another very important reason why garden wildlife needs to be taken more seriously. It's so accessible. From a purely scientific point of view, most of the great discoveries of the natural world have been made by patient and continuous observation. Where better to study wildlife than right outside your back door? Oddly enough, most naturalists of the past seem to have preferred less convenient places for their study. They apparently had a need to stand up to their waist in mud for weeks on end, or to be half eaten alive by insects, in order to give their work scientific credibility. As a result of that the supposedly familiar wildlife you can expect to attract into your garden is quite often less well understood than the more celebrated rare species of the tropical swamp or the frozen tundra.

Of course, I don't expect everyone to be interested in years of careful monitoring of snail movement, or the feeding preference of the cabbage white butterfly. For most of us the great joy of the accessibility which garden wildlife offers, is that we can become familiar with the plants and animals living on our doorsteps. We can see how they change from season to season, and the closer we look, and the more familiar we become, the deeper will be our commitment to helping nature to survive into the future. Garden wildlife is there to be enjoyed, certainly, but it has a job to do too. It is the wild plants and animals that we learn to love on our doorsteps, in our own gardens, that will lead more and more people to demand much greater care for the rare and precious wildlife which most of us will never see, but which we must do everything possible to conserve for the future.

Chapter 3

Planning the garden as a habitat for you and your wildlife

DON'T IMAGINE you need a five acre country estate before you can begin to plan for wildlife. Even a window box can provide a welcome resting place for passing butterflies if you grow the right flowers, and every tower block has its high rise nature lovers, tempting bluetits up to the tenth storey with bags of peanuts and lumps of fat. A friend of mine in Holland has a sand dune, a chalk grassland and an acid bog, each full of appropriate wildflowers, and all on a terrace just a few feet square. He has created exactly the right soil and drainage conditions for each community – in a set of concrete plant tubs. Every July he looks forward to the mammoth task of harvesting his hay meadow with a pair of kitchen scissors.

Don't feel either, that you can only start wildlife gardening if you are able to begin with a virgin plot. There is scope for a little more wildlife habitat in the most mature of gardens. My own patch was first laid out in 1907, and the lawn had been mown to within an inch of its life throughout every summer for the past seventy odd years. When I moved in, I decided to leave half the grass uncut for the first summer and see what happened. Within weeks there were sheets of wildflowers blooming. Lady's smock or the cuckoo flower popped up everywhere. Its delicate pink flowers pulled in lots of spring butterflies and I was thrilled to see handsome orange-tips feeding on the nectar, mating and then laying their eggs on the leaves of this lovely wildflower – all within a month or two of my moving in.

Let us suppose for a minute, though, that yours is a brand new garden on a new estate. Every plot will be different – different aspects, different climate, different soil – and of course you and your family will be different from everyone else. The most important thing about garden design is to begin by getting it right for *you*. Sort out the spaces *you* need, and then wildlife can be encouraged by building, planting and managing

Wildlife Gardens are for people. Create comfortable spaces where you can sit and relax – happy habitats for humans. Then you can begin to think about providing homes for wildlife too.

In a typical small suburban garden, there should be room for you and a wide range of wildlife habitats. Here, the beginnings of a woodland glade are developing with woodland edge, wildflower meadow, garden pond and cottage garden service station.

those spaces in particularly sympathetic ways.

I always find it is helpful to imagine the new garden first of all as a solid block of foam rubber – or in our case a solid patch of woodland. What you must then do is think about the spaces; the clearings you want to carve out of the solid. Ideally, if you have room, it is a good plan to imagine leaving a belt of solid woodland around the edge of your garden, to provide shelter, to screen you from the neighbours, and to give the more timid wildlife a secluded access route around, in and out of your garden. You will almost certainly want one space carving out in which you can sit and enjoy the sunshine, and if that can be close to the house then so much the better – you will be able to eat outside, too. That space probably needs to be the size of an average kitchen. Any bigger and it will be draughty and you will begin to feel uncomfortable. When the weather is hot, it's nice to have a place in the garden where you can sit in the shade too. This can be a tiny space just big enough to fit in a bench. If it is tucked under the canopy of your enclosing solid 'woodland', then it will also provide you with the ideal spot for sitting quietly and watching wildlife. Here the solid bank of imaginary trees and shrubs will help with your camouflage, and after a couple of minutes the birds you are watching will forget all about you.

24

Once you've sorted out the right spots for your sitting spaces, and you've worked out how big, or rather how small, they need to be, you can begin to think about carving out some bigger spaces. With a small town garden you may be left with just enough room for one central open space. Having tucked a patio into the sunniest corner, and a bench under the shrubbery facing towards the west, you will want to carve out a 'clearing' to look into. If the garden is bigger you might be able to carve out two or more central spaces, and these glades can perhaps be put to different uses. The one nearest the house might simply be a formal velvet lawn, neat, tidy and pretty to look at, useful for parties, but not much good for wildlife. You may then need another lawn-filled glade where the children can kick a ball about: rougher grass, scope for dandelions, starlings and daddylonglegs, but a bit too much activity for the more timid wild creatures. A third space might be devoted to vegetable growing, screened from the house but open to the sun, and a fourth glade could be developed specifically as a wildlife habitat, with the 'lawn' managed as wildflower meadow, a pool in the centre for frogs and dragonflies, and plenty of native wildflowers and rotting leaves to help encourage the mini-beasts.

If you really think about the garden as a series of outdoor rooms,

Even the smallest of back yards can house a lot of wildlife. Ivy against the wall shelters nesting birds; a pile of rotting logs is just the place for toads to lurk; and batboxes and birds' nesting boxes make up for the lack of large, old trees. Obviously a birdbath and birdtable will fit into the tiniest space.

enclosed by banks of shrubbery and woodland edge, then as your family demands change, the use of the spaces can be adjusted. When the children grow out of the football phase the goalposts can be removed and meadow flowers can be planted in their mini-Wembley. If the structure of the garden is right, and the various glades are comfortable for you, then your garden will be adaptable and the structure itself can form the bulk of your garden wildlife habitat.

Now let's think specifically about that wildlife glade, and remember if you are as keen as I am on wildlife in the garden, there's nothing to stop you devoting several 'glades' to habitat creation. Again the emphasis needs to be on *you* and your enjoyment of the wildlife. One sure way of providing plenty of activity in your wildlife glade the whole year round is to incorporate some water. If you can possibly manage it, invest in a big, shallow-edged pond. The wet margin could provide you with ideal growing conditions for a mass of very beautiful wildflowers, the water surface itself will reflect every subtle change in the weather, and within and around the pond there will be a constant buzz of activity. You will have flocks of starlings enjoying noisy January bathing parties, amorous frogs singing away on moonlit April evenings, spectacular dragonflies darting jerkily from one corner to another, and foxes, hedgehogs and all the other passing wildlife dropping in for a late-night drink. Try to make sure that part of the pond can be seen from the house. From my desk I can look across the patio and my flower-garden lawn to the water's edge, and whenever I glance up I am rewarded with some wildlife spectacle or another.

The other wildlife activity centre which you need to place in full view is the bird table. This needs to be out in the open anyway, to reduce the risk from pouncing cats, and if you feed regularly through the winter you really can attract a terrific variety of beautiful wild creatures to entertain you just a few feet from your window.

The rest of the open space within your 'glade' is likely to be lawn. Britain has a marvellous climate for growing grasslands. The traditional close-mown sward is OK for a few wildlife species. Daisies and plantains love it, for instance. Starlings and thrushes are happy hunting over it for the leatherjackets that feed on the grass roots, or the earthworms that tunnel away just below the surface. To increase the amount of wildlife it is well worth managing some of your lawn as a meadow. If it is big enough you may even arrange to have a spring flower meadow full of cowslips and lady's smock, which you mow as normal from July onwards, and a taller hay meadow coloured with lady's bedstraw, knapweed and scabious which you harvest in September. Do make sure that you keep some of your grassland mown neatly though. A close-cropped path through the meadow will help you get close to the wildlife without trampling down the taller plants, and a nice crisp edge to the

Even in a tiny town-house garden, the same basic rules apply – lots of cover from dense planting, and a grassy glade to catch the sunlight.

OPPOSITE, TOP: You must have somewhere comfortable and quiet to sit. As you blend into the background the wild creatures of the garden will lose their shyness and you will gain even more pleasure from your wildlife garden.

OPPOSITE, BOTTOM: Think of your wildlife garden as a woodland glade. A sheltered clearing in the forest is perhaps one of the richest of natural habitats. Your own personal glade can be further improved with 'service station' plants, too.

rather unorthodox 'hayfield' reassures your friends and neighbours. They are much more likely to accept your argument that 'it's meant to look like that!'

The bank of vegetation – all that is left of your carved up 'foam rubber' – which surrounds the glade should be made of a mixture of woodland edge habitat and service station flower garden. Keep the southern enclosure fairly low, to allow in plenty of sunshine, and do give yourself wide enough borders to be able to stack up the planting in a series of layers. Beware of putting in trees that will grow very big. It is always a painful decision when they have to come out later, and for most small gardens it is probably better to go for large shrubs such as hawthorn, Buddleia and field maple instead. Build somewhere into your 'woodland edge' where you can hide the compost heap. It may be marvellous for wildlife but it's not likely to look very pretty, and it can pong a bit in mid-summer. If you don't have enough room for a 'woodland edge' border around the whole of your glade, then shuffle the whole thing over and use a hedge to form one of the boundaries – perhaps the southern or eastern one. This will allow in the sun, give you space on the opposite edge for a more generous bank of shrubs, and will give you yet another slightly different habitat.

Sometimes when you move into a brand new garden you arrive before the topsoil. Sometimes the topsoil never arrives. If you do have a choice, then it is worth thinking about soil fertility in relation to your garden layout. Ideally you want maximum growth in the vegetable patch where you are hoping to grow crops, and along the lines of structure planting – the woodland edge and shrub borders – where you are hoping for rapid growth to provide shelter. Use up the topsoil in these areas. Your formal lawns and flower beds need an inch or two of topsoil to keep them looking green through the summer, but your meadow will perform best on very poor soil. The ideal material for the centre of your glade is fast-draining sandy subsoil. If your meadow is on deep, rich topsoil then the grasses will grow like mad, and the colourful meadow wildflowers will be swamped out of existence.

Finally, if you have a choice, go for a garden plot with a variation of levels. Basically you are aiming to attract a wide and interesting diversity of wildlife. That will be easiest if your garden contains a variety of subtly different variations on the habitat theme, and a garden with sloping banks, damp hollows and well-drained plateaux will automatically provide that diversity.

Most of us have gardens which already have a history. Indeed I expect for most people wildlife gardening will simply be a new phase in the life of a garden they have been living with for years. If that is the situation you are in, then you will be looking for painless ways of improving the wildlife habitat without any dramatic, radical upheaval. Again, as a first

rule I repeat my plea to relax. There is a whole host of ways in which you can subtly change the management of your garden to benefit wildlife. Raise the lawnmower blades an inch higher and your formal lawn will improve dramatically as a habitat for insects and creeping wildflowers. Accumulate a stockpile of dead logs, plant prunings and fallen leaves, and the small mammals will thrive. Leave flowerheads to run to seed and flocks of finches will feed there through the winter. Have faith in the balance of nature instead of relying on chemical poison to tackle the garden pests – in no time at all you'll have lacewings, ladybirds, toads and hedgehogs galore.

Once you've adopted the right, relaxed, 'ecologically sympathetic' attitude and learned to love a little untidiness, you can begin building up the wildlife service station aspect of your garden. This can be done gradually and cheaply. Erect a bird table and put out food regularly. Put up a few well-sited nestboxes for the small birds and perhaps a batbox or two. Introduce more and more garden flowers which are good pollen, nectar and seed producers, and add some native plants to the shrub and flower borders. Grow climbers up the fences and walls, choosing natives such as honeysuckle and old man's beard in preference to 'foreigners', and allow the existing shrubberies to grow up and provide the sheltering

With a large garden you really can create quite a nature reserve. Concentrate your efforts in the quieter corners and provide a sanctuary with lots of native planting and safe shelter. The vegetable patch should have flowers planted in it and your wildlife pesticide squad of owls, hoverflies, hedgehogs, ladybirds, songthrushes and slow-worms will fight it out with the caterpillars, slugs and snails. You may have foxes living under your garden shed and grass-snakes breeding in your compost heap.

Relaxation is the watch-
word. Wildlife gardening
should give you plenty of
time to lie back, close your
eyes, and enjoy the sounds
and scents of your own little
patch of countryside.

Remember you are designing
your wildlife garden so that
you can enjoy it. Concentrate
your cottage garden planting
close to the house; position
service station facilities such
as the birdtable and the pond
in full view and allow a more
relaxed countryside
atmosphere to develop at the
far end of the garden.

Concentrate the 'service-station' planting of cottage-garden flowers close to the house. A wildlife garden certainly does not need to be a 'wilderness'.

canopy for lower-growing layers of groundcover and shade-loving wildflowers. Gradually, as the emphasis in the garden changes, you will be rewarded with more and more wildlife visitors.

Once the popularity of your service station wildlife garden is established, you will have a regular stream of summer butterflies dropping in from the local railway embankment to top up with nectar, and the neighbourhood hedgehog family paying nightly summer visits for their saucer of bread and milk and their chemical-free slugs and earthworms. This is the time to think about rich habitat gardening – actually providing complete habitats which allow wild plants and animals to set up permanent homes in your garden. Some lucky people have gardens big enough to accommodate a badger sett, or breeding sparrowhawks, but for most of us the scale of habitat our garden offers will be much more modest.

Given the choice, I would go for the wetland habitat first. They are the most exciting for me, and they show thrilling results almost instantly. Within two hours of my filling our pond, pondskaters and whirlygig beetles had flown in to investigate. If you have small children, then you may feel a pond is a bit hazardous, though there is a school of thought which suggests that the best way to teach children to respect water is to have them grow up with it. A wildlife gardener friend of mine in Switzerland stood casually on one side whilst his two-year-old son took stock of their new pond. Inevitably the infant rushed straight down into the shallow water, got the shock of his life and was whisked to safety by his dad. He's treated water with great caution ever since. If, however, you are not too keen on amateur child psychology, then I suggest you go for a different kind of wetland. Dig a pond, line it and fill it in again to make a wetland marsh. You'll still be able to grow wonderful plants such as ragged robin and marsh marigold, and when the family is ready for a real pond you can simply dig a hole in the middle of your nicely established marsh. In fact, that is a very good way of making use of any old leaking concrete pond you may inherit.

There are a whole range of different detailed habitats to have a go at once you get the bug. You can plant more and more wildflowers into your developing meadow, stack piles of logs in your woodland edge, and if you want a real splash of summer colour, one of the most instantaneous habitats you can create is a cultivated 'weed' patch. Many of our more spectacular wildflowers are short-lived annuals. Flowers like the poppy, cornflower, corncockle, corn marigold, heartsease and mayweed are adapted to grow best in disturbed ground. Remember their original habitat would have been on river shingle, or collapsed stream cliffs. For generations they competed with farmers' crops, and produced the chocolate-box country landscapes we dream about. Nowadays modern herbicides have made it very easy to wipe out the cornfield wildflowers.

Indeed corncockle is virtually extinct in Britain, though many of the other, more adaptable species have side-stepped from farmland on to the disturbed ground of motorway construction sites and building excavations. The seeds of all these species germinate very easily in spring. The flowers bloom right through the summer, and it only takes a little light raking of the soil surface at the end of the summer for their crop of fresh seed to germinate to give you a repeat performance the following year. The blaze of colour produced by even the smallest patch of cornfield weeds will excite all those who visit your garden, and will probably be the aspect of wildlife gardening they find most immediately understandable.

There is one more consideration you need to bear in mind when designing or redesigning your wildlife garden. Have a good look at your neighbourhood. The animal life you are able to attract into your garden will be influenced a great deal by the broader landscape in which you live. The richer the wildlife is in the surrounding area, the more 'passing trade' you can expect to attract into your service station. If you do live next door to a large patch of urban wild-scape – an old demolition site or a gravel pit for example – then you will have far more chance of attracting clouds of butterflies to your buddleia than those wildlife gardeners who live on the edge of a rural village, with a plot which backs on to acres of chemically managed arable crops. The reason my pond was colonised so quickly, I imagine, had a great deal to do with the number of relatively unpolluted ponds and reservoirs there are in my neighbourhood. If you have a wood nearby, then your bird table may attract the attention of such spectacular creatures as spotted woodpeckers and nuthatches as well as a constant stream of dozens of individual bluetits, coaltits, great-tits and other small woodland birds. There is an old oakwood quite near here which has green woodpeckers breeding in it. These handsome birds love feeding on ants, and in the early morning they can often be seen feeding on the nearby suburban lawns, dabbing up garden ants with their incredibly long tongues.

Obviously you may choose to create a habitat which is completely alien to the area in the belief that this will diversify the wildlife of the neighbourhood. There is nothing to stop you creating an acid peat-bog community, or an alkaline sand dune if you want, though watering your sand dune with salty water every couple of days can pall after a while. I must say, though, that I think it is much better to go for garden habitats which complement the local wildlife community. For one thing, an isolated island of peat bog in the heart of suburbia is never likely to be anything more than a collection of plants. The appropriate animal life simply won't be around to colonise it. Conversely, if you create a mini-habitat typical of the area you are likely to be very successful at attracting wildlife to join you. Create a small patch of 'chalk downland' in your back garden now, while there are still a few acres up the road, or dig a pond and plant up a marsh while the local mill pond is still full of water. The meadow butterfly population will quickly expand to adopt your mini-downland. The diving beetles, insects and dragonflies will drop into your mini-wetland in no time, and who knows, in a year or two's time the original habitat may be destroyed, leaving you with the only facility in the area capable of sustaining the local wildlife. This may seem fanciful but it has certainly been the case with amphibians such as frogs and newts. Populations have been virtually wiped out in many rural counties, but garden ponds have provided a viable substitute for the lost farm ponds and ditches.

It is not just *existing* local habitats that you need to think about either. Most of us have a park or some other 'official open space' close to where we live. Imagine how much more successful your mini-meadow is likely to be if you can persuade the local park keepers to adopt the same kind of wildlife management on a few acres of their municipal greenery. Use a bit of gentle persuasion and you could have lots of local authority butterflies, skylarks and kestrels paying visits to your wildlife garden.

PART 2
Creating New Habitats

ABOVE: The meadow brown butterfly, and
several of its 'brown' relatives, must have
the stems of grasses in their breeding
habitat. This one laid its eggs in my new
meadow the very first summer.

Chapter 4

Shrubberies ~
the woodland edge habitat

OPPOSITE: Many of our garden
wild plants and animals are
refugees from the primeval
forest landscape. A mini
woodland edge will therefore
provide a home for a wide
range of attractive species.
Fox, badger and squirrel may
appear in larger gardens.
Robins love garden habitat.
Siskins will spend the winter
with you if you plant alder.
Native trees and shrubs are
important for the insects they
support. Mountain ash, wild
rose, honeysuckle and elder
are all valuable. Small
songbirds enjoy this habitat –
garden warbler, bluetit, great-
tit and wren. The speckled
wood butterfly and the
comma both spend the
summer sunbathing in the
dappled shade. Woodmice,
hedgehogs and toads forage
in the leaf-litter. Predators
such as the stoat will follow
the woodland edge when
moving from garden to
garden in search of prey.

SHRUBBERIES HAVE been a feature of modern gardens ever since the end of the last century. They provide shelter, screen unsightly corners and make an attractive backdrop for the garden flowers. Your wildlife garden needs all these things, too. This, remember, is the bank of foam rubber which has been left behind after you have carved out your garden 'rooms'. With a little adjustment, you can turn your traditional garden shrubbery into a really valuable wildlife habitat. You can create a woodland edge around your garden glade.

I have already explained that many of our favourite garden wildlife species originally lived in the forests. Ever since the ancient Britons started farming we have been chopping down our trees, grubbing up our woodlands, and generally reducing woodland habitat. In recent years the rate of destruction has been greater than ever. We have destroyed more of our ancient woodlands in the past forty years than our ancestors managed to wipe out in the previous four hundred. In that same forty years it is true that we have also planted a great many trees, but the vast majority of those are exotic, sombre conifers, and you only need to walk from the song-filled, dappled shade of a deciduous copse into the silent gloom of a softwood plantation to know immediately that, in wildlife terms, conifers are comparatively lifeless. Much of the woodland wildlife that thrived in our oak and beech woods up to the turn of the century has suffered too, because there has been a dramatic change in the woodland habitat. The trees may still be there, but the sheets of primroses and the clouds of butterflies that used to share your woodland walk have gone. They relied on regular management of the wood. Coppicing in particular produced a very rich habitat for wildlife. Whilst the tall trees may have grown unhindered for hundreds of years, local people would cut down the understorey – perhaps hazel, hornbeam or lime – every ten or fifteen years. That practice had gone on for centuries, providing firewood,

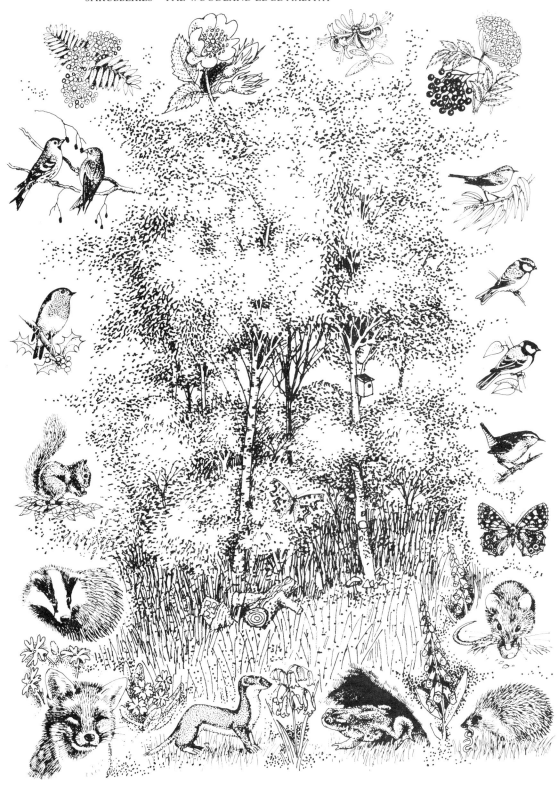

Our native shrubs are very beautiful, and far better for wildlife than exotic garden introductions. What could be more delicately beautiful than the sweet-scented dog-rose (*Rosa canina*, opposite, top), or more colourful than the autumn bunches of berries on the guelder-rose (*Viburnum opulus*, opposite, bottom).

fenceposts, hedging stakes and small wood for every possible local use, and at the same time creating an extremely rich habitat for a wide variety of plants and animals. In just two generations this intensive but sensitive creative management has disappeared. Such coppicing only survives as a quaint country craft around the odd folk museum or in very special nature reserves. Most of our ancient woodland now has a tangle of bramble, overgrown or collapsed coppice shrubs, and a forest of light-trapping sycamore seedlings as its impenetrable undergrowth, and whilst the wrens and the blackbirds still thrive, the nightingale misses the light openness of the hazel coppice, and primroses have become very rare indeed.

If you are lucky enough to have a good wood which still survives in your area, and the local County Naturalists Trust will almost certainly be taking care of one or two, go along and have a wander through it. In fact you should really go along several times in the course of a year, and see just how excitingly it changes from season to season. As you become familiar with your woodland community you will pick up a good many clues about how the habitat works. Perhaps the most encouraging thing you will notice is how important the edges are. Where the trees and shrubs end and the sunlight breaks through, you find more species of plant and animals than anywhere else in the wood. It is not surprising if you think about it. You have a chance of seeing species which live deep in the shade of the wood, and species that prefer the open sunlight but perhaps cling to the woodland edge for protection. There are also a host of special plants and animals that actually like the half-shade best of all. The posh word for this ecological boundary line is an 'ecotone', but I like to think of it as a wildlife bonus zone.

Hardly anyone has room in their garden for a complete woodland, though there are a few lucky people who live on the edge of a real one. But even in a small garden you can have a go at creating the richest bit of the woodland habitat – the bonus zone. Of course without the whole of the wood to back it up you are not likely to have badger cubs crashing out of the bramble-patch to gambol in your meadow, or a startled deer blinking at you in the surprise of the sunshine. You can grow all the woodland edge wildflowers, though, and you'll certainly have lots of small mammals and songbirds moving into the habitat once it becomes established. Woodland edge is particularly good for butterflies, too. I remember cycling along on a holiday in France one year, with woodland down to the road on each side. At ten o'clock each morning the sun came up over the tree-tops, the ditch full of wildflowers was suddenly bathed in light, and within a few warming minutes the whole habitat was alive with dancing butterflies. In my garden there are three species of butterfly that seem to enjoy the woodland edge best. Speckled woods are perfectly camouflaged in the dappled shade. Commas sunbathe happily with

38

orange wings outstretched on the bramble leaves, until you get too close, when they snap shut and the dull, camouflaged underside of their wings makes them disappear. Gatekeeper, or wall-brown butterflies are the third species and they presumably got their country name because they so often flutter around the hawthorn and honeysuckle growing where the field-gate punctures the darkness on the edge of the wood.

There are three simple principles you need to adopt if you are going to create a successful woodland-edge habitat. You must develop several layers of plants one above the other; you must include a good range of native plants, from trees down to carpeting wildflowers; and you must build up a rich layer of dead and decaying material, from big logs to fine leaf mould.

The multiple canopy idea is a good one to adopt, even if you're simply growing exotic plants in your garden. Apart from the ecological value, it helps you fit more plants into a given space. Each of the layers will provide a home for different species of wildlife. If you watch closely you will see that your garden birds are really quite specific about the layer in which they operate. The songthrush, the wood pigeon and the long-tailed tits tend to stick to the tree-tops. The finches and the robin seem to prefer the shrub layer, and wrens, dunnocks and blackbirds spend most of their time among the leaf litter or in the very low vegetation.

In a real wood, each canopy of plants helps create the particular climatic conditions which the plants in the layer below enjoy best. When you are starting from scratch you have to concertina the process, and actually choose the plants that will thrive in their particular canopy layer. The choice becomes more and more critical, the nearer you get to ground level and the less light there is available. The other problem, of course, is that it takes time for the various trees, shrubs and flowers to grow into their respective layers, and you may well be able to grow sun-loving shrubs such as broom and gorse in your woodland edge for several years, until the trees eventually grow up and overshadow them.

It is important to grow at least one tree, even in the smallest garden. Trees presumably help to let birds and insects know that yours is a green service station garden, and there is something very special about planting something which will live longer than us, and grow much taller. If you have plenty of room, plant lots of trees. Plant them small. Certainly they should never be bigger than a couple of metres tall. Put them in about three metres apart. This allows you plenty of space for planting the other layers, but at the same time, the trees will be close enough together to force one another up and produce a canopy of leaves and branches on most soils within three or four years. Look for a good, healthy, fibrous root system, and it is also most important to choose trees which have a good central shoot growing vigorously upwards. All too often the trees in nurseries and garden centres have had the growing tip, or central leader,

NATIVE TREES SUITABLE FOR THE AVERAGE GARDEN

Silver birch (*Betula pendula*) A pretty tree with small leaves, weeping branches, silvery bark and casting a light shade. A rough texture in the young shoots usually indicates good bark colour to follow. Prefers well-drained, open conditions – poor soil if possible. Ultimate height 20 metres, and a healthy life span of 50–60 years. Old trees good for bracket fungi and attractive to woodpeckers. Propagate from seed. 229 associated insect species.

Downy birch (*Betula pubescens*) A 'darker' tree, with downy twigs, but growing better where soil is moist to wet. Over 200 associated insect species.

Hawthorn (*Crataegus monogyna*) Well worth growing as a specimen for its display of white May-blossom and the rich crop of bright red berries. It is thorny and very tough, though not always easy to establish at first. 149 associated insect species.

Alder (*Alnus glutinosa*) Grown best in wet soils, where it produces a tall, slender, rather dark tree up to 15 metres tall. It is a nitrogen-fixer, and its purple catkins in spring produce clouds of pollen and fertilise the cone-like female flowers. A popular seed-source for siskins and other small birds in the autumn and winter. Very tolerant of air pollution. 90 associated insect species.

Aspen poplar (*Populus tremmula*) A lovely small tree with constantly fluttering leaves which turn brilliant gold in the autumn. Prefers a moist, neutral to acid soil but will grow in the most exposed of positions. Over 90 associated insect species.

Rowan (*Sorbus aucuparia*) Bunches of white blossom in spring, and a mass of orange berries from September onwards make this a very useful decorative tree. It grows well in very exposed positions and will reach 15 metres. 28 species of associated insects.

Crab apple (*Malus sylvestris*) Pink blossom, green or golden fruit and a spreading, characterful habit. There are lots of exotic species and hybrids, but do try and choose the native crab. This may be one to propagate for yourself from a local hedgerow specimen. Over 90 associated insect species.

The following forest-size trees are too tall for most gardens, but they can all be grown as coppiced specimens, or incorporated into a mixed hedge.

Oaks (*Quercus robur* and *Q. petrea*) have 284 species of associated insects.

Beech (*Fagus sylvatica*) supports 64 species.

Ash (*Fraxinus excelsior*) supports 41 species.

White willow (*Salix alba*) supports over 200 species.

Elm (*Ulmus procera*) supports 80 species.

Small leaved lime (*Tilia cordata*) supports 31 species.

Hornbeam (*Carpinus betulus*) supports 28 species.

Wild cherry or Gean (*Prunus avium*) is also excellent, though figures are not available.

NOTE: popular species such as
Sycamore (*Acer pseudoplatanus*)
Norway maple (*Acer platanoides*)
Horse chestnut (*Aesculus hippocastaenum*)
Sweet chestnut (*Castanea sativa*)
The tree of heaven (*Ailanthus alata*) and
Japanese cherries (*Prunus japonica*)
are none of them native and they support very few species of insects.

cut out. The grower does this to encourage the sapling to produce a bunch of side shoots. This may make the young plant look more like a tree, but it can prevent it from growing up to form a natural shape. Trees in the wild rarely have their branches starting only six feet up the trunk.

Eventually, trees planted three metres apart will become overcrowded, and you will have to cut some of them down, but I think this is better than waiting years and years for the tree canopy to develop. Little trees are really cheap. They don't need staking, and they grow so fast that normally they will overtake the much more expensive standard trees within the second year. I planted a group of silver birch in my last garden. They went in at just over a metre tall, and five years later they were as high as a two-storey house.

Once the trees have been planted – and the best times of year to plant most woody species are either late autumn, just after leaf-fall, or early spring, just before bud-burst – then you can think about inter-planting with the shrubs. These will form the second layer down. If you've lots of room you may even be able to fit in a range of species which will give you a two-tier shrub layer. In fact in some really good, old woodlands you can find three layers of shrubs below the high tree canopy.

A lovely wood near me has tall, multi-stemmed lime and rowan trees reaching up to the lower branches of the oaks, with hazel and bird cherry below that, and a bottom layer of bramble and wild rose. Below that there is a sheet of spring flowers. Bluebells, primroses and the rest all flower early enough to have been fertilised by the insects, produced ripe seed and their leaves will usually have begun to die back before the shrubs and trees above them cut out all the sun. In the garden you should plant shrubs at about one metre spacings, and then cut them hard back. Chop them down to a few inches if you can bring yourself to do it. This encourages them to produce dense low growth and form a shrub layer very quickly.

If you are planting a woodland-edge habitat from scratch, then I suggest you concentrate on establishing the tree and shrub layer for the first year or two. Once the shade begins to develop you can start introducing the wildflowers. In the first couple of seasons there will still be wide gaps between the trees and shrubs, and of course every gardener knows that is an invitation for weeds to grow. It may come as a bit of a surprise to find that you need to control weeds in a wildlife garden, but I don't really want a tangle of sowthistle and groundsel choking my tree and shrub planting, any more than the next person. Naturally I'm keen to avoid using chemical weedkillers if possible, though I must admit there are a few over-enthusiastic weeds like ground elder and couchgrass that do get a dab of systemic contact weedkiller gel, even in my garden. I find the best way to avoid most of the weed problem, however, is to spread a mulch over the soil surface. If you can get it, or afford to buy it, the best material, particularly in the woodland-edge habitat, is 75–100mm chunks of coarsely chopped tree bark. Alternatively, although it doesn't look, feel or smell quite so woodlandy, a metre square of roofing felt, or even a sheet of cardboard or carpet around the base of each plant will suppress the weeds and keep the soil moisture up around the roots. There are a lot of finer textured materials sold as mulches – pulverised bark, peat, and mushroom compost – but they all create problems if you use them, because windborne weed seed germinates on the surface, and the little seedlings grow like mad with their roots down in the mulch.

Chopped bark can also form the first instalment of your introduction of dead wood and decaying material to your woodland edges. This really is a vitally important part of woodland habitat. So many of the small woodland creatures spend at least part of their life munching through dead wood or hiding under damp logs. I was very lucky when I made my wildlife garden for TV. All along one boundary there had been a row of majestic old elm trees. Sadly they succumbed to the dreaded Dutch elm disease several years before I arrived on the scene, and had been chopped down. In fact, the regrowth of elm suckers is now about five metres tall, and just beginning to suffer from a second dose of the disease. Anyway the previous owners had kept a good many of the big slices of tree trunk, and used them for garden stools, pergola bases, and anything else they could think of. I heaved several of these logs into two or three piles,

Decay is a vital part of the woodland habitat. My bank of dead logs provides a home for a wide range of fascinating plants and animals (and perhaps the odd wood-sprite, too.)

carefully positioned where they would be safe from disturbance. I also used another dozen or so of them to retain a bank of soil in the woodland edge. The first autumn I was rewarded with a spectacular display of fungi of all shapes and sizes – neat spherical pink blobs and big tough brown brackets: at one point my woodland edge looked like a bit of Walt Disney fairyland. The toadstools are just the fruiting part of the fungi, of course, and although most of them perform in autumn, there are usually one or two in evidence most of the year. If you can accumulate logs from a variety of different types of tree, then you will discover that their fungi vary, too. The bulk of the fungus (the mycelium) is below the surface, extending deep down into the dead tissue of the rotting logs. It helps break it down to a soft pulp which other organisms are then more easily able to digest. For the most part, fungi are harmless in the garden, just a useful and interesting part of the natural recycling process – the ecological balance I've talked about. One or two species of toadstool are poisonous, and it is as well to have a book or chart somewhere in the house, where you can check suspicious-looking growths for safety. Failing this, simply adopt the policy that *all* toadstools are likely to be nasty to eat, and are best left to the wildlife. Incidentally, I've been amazed at just how much wildlife the fungi do attract. There are famous examples of the very smelly toadstool species such as the stinkhorn which are irresistible to flies. They zoom in from the neighbourhood, crawl around on the evil-smelling green jelly which covers the tip of the toadstools and, of course, in so doing pick up spores which they then cart off somewhere else. My elm logs have been particularly good for producing big, brown, striped bracket fungi in both spring and autumn, and these in turn have been the focus of attention for slugs and snails, which seem to delight in crawling around all over them, chewing off great lumps. Each morning the fungus looks more and more 'got-at' and all around it on the log there is a tell-tale network of silvery snail trails.

There is another hazard presented by all this decay, and it is only fair to mention it. There is one fungus, *Armillaria mellea*, the honey fungus, which can grow on dead logs *and* attack and kill living trees and shrubs. It sends out long underground threads or hyphae from the infected dead log, and enters the living tree through the roots. The victim is killed as the fungus blocks up the transport system, the tubes inside the plant. The underground threads are black and very tough, and give *Armillaria* its other popular name of bootlace fungus. This fungus is really very common. It is probably present in every wood in Britain, and in a great many gardens, too. Most of the time it does no harm at all, but if there are big, old, sickly trees around, then honey fungus does seem to be attracted to them, and can provide the last lethal blow. Generally speaking, vigorous, healthy specimens are not affected, but just occasionally there seems to be a change in the fungus, it acts more aggressively, and there are certainly gardens around where several trees and shrubs have been killed in a short space of time. The fungus produces its toadstools in September. They are about 40mm across, golden yellow with a slightly darker brown colour in the centre of the 'cap' and they pop up in clusters at the base of infected trees and logs.

It is obviously important to be aware of risks such as this. Frankly, though, wildlife gardening is much less hazardous than intensive chemical gardening. The balance you find in woodland seems to help reduce the impact of honey fungus there to a modest, almost insignificant level, and it's reasonable to suppose that the same will be true in your garden. Most people know that penicillin is a fungus which is very successful at suppressing the effect of other, harmful fungi, and it could well be that one or other of the many different toadstools found in a wood, or in your new woodland edge habitat, may have a similar influence over the deadly bootlace. In any event, however neat and tidy you are in your garden, there is still plenty of scope for this fungus to affect you. So far as infectious dead wood is concerned, a gate post or fence post is just as good a host as your pile of carefully selected logs. On balance I'm happy to take the risk. I keep an eye out for honey fungus toadstools each autumn, and as a precaution I've positioned the pond between my log piles and a lovely old apple tree which I think might be particularly vulnerable. In all honesty, though, I know that if an extra vigorous strain of honey fungus does visit my garden there is really little I can do, and all the other fascinating toadstools, insects and organisms of decay my woodland edge attracts are more than enough compensation for the slight risk I'm taking.

You can expect masses of animal life to make use of your dead wood, too. There are a great many insects and other invertebrates which actually tunnel away inside the logs. Many beetles in particular spend their larval stage there. The elm logs in my garden are full of big, squidgy, white grubs, anything up to 20mm long. I found the first few when I was splitting a spare log for the fire, and that persuaded me that the more rotten, soft-centred lumps of timber should definitely be reserved for the wildlife. I've since discovered that these are the grubs of the lesser stag beetle, and in fact when I turn over a log in my woodland edge there are usually a couple of handsome, dull black adults lying there on their backs, slowly waving their legs in the air and looking very disgruntled by my rude disturbance. The logs I used to retain the earthbank are full of insect life too. All through the summer there is a constant coming and going of tiny black flying creatures. Sit and watch carefully for a few minutes and you will see that the logs are peppered with neat little holes. These insects are woodwasps of various types, which lay their eggs in the tunnels which they or some other creatures have dug. Some of the wasps have an amazing ability to fly straight into their tunnel at breakneck

A great many creatures depend on dead wood for survival. Here a tell-tale pile of 'sawdust' shows that some beetle or woodwasp is busy tunnelling away inside the log.

speed. Other species seem rather less foolhardy, landing beside the hole first, and then reversing cautiously in, presumably preparing to lay an egg. Their caution is sensible, too, because quite often the hole they have chosen is already occupied, and they come whizzing out rather more quickly than they went in.

Much larger creatures use the log piles too. It generally stays damp and cool under the logs, and so quite a lot of moisture-loving animals hide there during the day, and then creep out after dark to hunt amongst the dew-covered damp vegetation. Slugs are commonplace, of course, though their variety of texture, colour and pattern deserves far more attention. The most fascinating creatures that shelter under my logs, though, are the young amphibians. Yearling newts in particular seem to love the damp conditions, and while the current season's newtlets are still sporting gills and darting jerkily about in the pond, the yearlings can be found huddled together under the logs. I've discovered anything up to fifteen young smooth newts under one elm log on some days, and the next day just one or two remained. This rather confirms the theory that they shelter there in the daytime, and move out to feed on lesser beasties after nightfall.

With so much life crawling in and around the dead wood of the woodland edge, it is not surprising that larger predators find it a useful place to visit, too. Garden spiders stake their claim almost the minute the logs hit the deck, and string up their beautiful webs in the hope of trapping the unfortunate wood wasps. Hunting spiders will move in too. My bark mulch and dead logs are alive with crowds of little black spiders which dart away as I approach. They are brilliantly camouflaged, and quite invisible – until they move. They don't build webs, but instead they make their living by lying in wait, and then pouncing on poor unsuspecting flies and creepy crawlies – the muggers in the log pile, so to speak. Fascinating, though. Look very closely at these apparently dull little grey spiders and in mid-summer you will find that some of them have what appears at first glance to be a knobbly back end. If the spider stands still long enough you will be able to recognise the knobbles are a mass of tiny baby spiders, carted around by their mother for safe-keeping.

Where there are spiders, you will often find wrens, and certainly I have a pair of these handsome, noisy little birds in my garden. A large part of their diet is spiders, and when they have a brood of chicks to feed they spend a great deal of their time hunting among the logs and flying back to the cluster of eager open mouths poking out from the nest hole in the eaves.

The wandering hedgehogs never fail to visit the logs. Blackbirds are forever pecking away at the soft ground beneath the edge of the pile, scattering bark in all directions in their frantic search for food, and even the local fox knows that it is worth turning the logs over from time to time, on the off-chance of picking up a wood mouse or one of my beautiful beetles.

TOP: Native plants are essential to the wildlife garden. Each plant species has its own array of dependent 'creepy-crawlies' and many of the grubs and caterpillars are very restricted in what they can eat. This buff-tip moth caterpillar eats the leaves of oak, birch and one or two other native shrubs.

BOTTOM: The adult buff-tip moth is perfectly camouflaged as a broken piece of birch twig.

★ ★ ★

Woodlands are not just full of dead wood, of course. They are a wonderful collection of living plants, too, and a great many species of animals live on leaves, flowers and fruits. So far as shelter and protection are concerned, any species of tree or shrub is useful, but to make the very best wildlife habitat you *must* plant native species. Remember that you are no longer interested simply in the way a plant *looks*. You're interested in the part it can play in attracting and supporting wildlife. It is a simple fact that the native animal life of any country depends fundamentally on native plants. In our case we have a complex, mixed community of wild plants and animals which have 'grown up together' since the last Ice Age, eight to ten thousand years ago. Not all our animal life feeds directly on plants, of course, but even the most carnivorous of predators feed on other animals which themselves feed on plants, or on other plant-eating creatures. The leaves and shrubs of native plants provide the basic platform for our animal life, and it is important to understand just how particular many of our lower forms of wildlife are about what they eat. Very many of the plant-eating insect larvae, for instance, only eat the leaves of one specific type of plant, and when that is the case, that plant will *always* be a native one. This is why it is so important to plant native trees, shrubs and wildflowers in your woodland edge, and indeed in every other wildlife habitat you create. The greater the variety of natives you include, the larger the menu you are providing, and the wider the range of animals you are likely to attract. Some species of plants support more different dependent leaf-eaters than others, and each species of plant will have its own special range of animal life. If you want to make a simple comparison, look at the oak trees you can buy in your garden centre.

The native English oaks, *Quercus petrea* and *Quercus robur*, are capable of providing a home for an amazing 284 different species of invertebrates – many of which can eat nothing else but English oak. By contrast, the America red oak, *Quercus rubra*, the cut-leaved, hairy acorned Turkey oak, *Quercus cerris*, and the evergreen holm oak, *Quercus ilex* can be eaten by no more than four or five species altogether. That is the situation here in Britain of course. Go to North America, Turkey or the Mediterranean where these exotic species grow as natives, and you find that there they support as wide a range of their own native fauna as our oaks do here.

In a good, healthy bit of garden wildlife habitat there will be hardly a leaf that has not had a bite taken out of it. Some of the smaller species actually live inside the leaves, and you can see thin wiggly lines snaking around beneath the surface. Look for these leaf miner tunnels particularly on bramble, holly and birch leaves, and on the leaves of woodland wildflowers such as red campion and primrose. The patterns are generally made by the caterpillars of tiny moths, and again they are often absolutely specific about which plant's leaves they can live in.

Other animals rely on your woodland edge plants, too. Not all of them are leaf-eaters. Many of the birds will be looking for seeds. Jays will gorge themselves on acorns in the autumn, and do a very good job of spreading them around too, when they bury them in soon-to-be-forgotten larders. Siskins are lovely little birds that look like slimmed-down greenfinches. They spend winter here and summer further north. They feed in flocks on the seed of English alder, and you can sometimes see twenty or thirty birds feeding together on cold January days. Look out for redpolls too – these pretty little birds often join the siskins in mixed feeding parties.

Even at the creepy-crawly end of the woodland wildlife community, seeds are an important food source. If you find an empty hazelnut with a small neat hole in it, then when you crack it open you will find the kernel has been eaten away by a small insect larva, and the hole is the point at which it left after the food ran out. The reason wildflowers such as foxglove and campion produce so many thousands of seed from each plant is that they need to compensate for the enormous majority that are eaten by something or other. There are quite complex specialisms too. The seeds of greater celandine and primrose are both covered with a waxy outer coating which ants seem to like eating. When the seeds are ripe the ants cart them away from the parent plant, strip off the delicious coating, and leave them in a bit of your woodland edge where they can germinate and grow, or perhaps be eaten by yet another creature.

In the panel on pages 52–3 there is a long list of native plants suitable for your woodland-edge habitat. Many of them are very beautiful. Being native they are unlikely to suffer in cold winters, and being part of the naturally balanced native community they are unlikely to be eaten to the point of destruction in the way that exotic plants sometimes are. Within the recommended three-layer structure you can pick and choose the plants you like best. For small gardens it is obviously sensible to avoid very big trees, or plants which spread like mad. You don't have to stick exclusively to natives either. You should now understand how critical it is to include some native plants, but there are masses of woodland shrubs and flowers from other countries that also enjoy this habitat. Some of the cotoneasters and berberis are very good seed producers, and plants like azaleas and mock orange are beautiful shrubs to have in any garden, filling the air with perfume and providing lots of pollen and nectar. Just bear in mind, however, that each time you plant an exotic instead of a native plant you are taking up a bit of space which could be supporting a greater diversity of wildlife.

There are several native plants which I think are particularly useful for garden woodland-edge habitat. Amongst the trees, silver birch (*Betula pendula*) is marvellous because it looks so beautiful in every season, its seeds are popular with tits in particular, its leaves feed interesting creatures like the birch saw-fly larva, and it casts a very light shade which makes it easy to grow other layers of plants beneath it. English alder (*Alnus glutinosa*), rowan (*Sorbus aucuparia*) and wild gean or cherry (*Prunus avium*) are the other tallish trees I would suggest you have a look at.

Coming down a layer there are lots of really attractive woodland-edge shrubs. Bird cherry (*Prunus padus*) is particularly handsome with its long plumes of white blossom covered in bees in the spring, and small cherries to feed the blackbirds and thrushes in autumn. Hazel is a must, with its lambs-tail catkins in the early spring and its cobnuts for the mice and squirrels in the autumn. My hazels also support a wonderful species of shield bug about the size of my little finger-nail and shiny brown and green. It spends a lot of its time sheltering from predators under those thick green leaf-sheaths that surround the hazelnuts and has an unusual characteristic for an insect – it protects its young. Hawthorn and field maple are always worth growing, if you have room, though they can be used to make a hedge instead, and wild dogrose is a plant I love to have in the garden. Its thorns are rather vicious but the flowers are so perfect, the rose hips are spectacular to look at and very popular with the birds, and if you are lucky you may find a robin's pincushion or two decorating the rose-twigs. These are actually galls which the rose is stimulated to produce by yet another little resident creature. Several eggs of this particular gall wasp are laid in a bud in the spring, and as the bright red 'pincushion' matures it provides a mini-habitat for a whole host of other even smaller creatures too. When the gall-fly larvae hatch they feed on the plant tissue that makes up the centre of the gall.

Down at ground level, the choice of native plants is enormous, and these shade-loving wildflowers really are some of the most beautiful things you could ever wish to grow. Most of them flower in spring to make use of the sunlight early in the year, before the trees and shrubs close canopy. Almost all are easy to grow from seed if you aren't able to buy them from a nursery. However tempting it might be you must *never* dig up wild plants for your garden. Fortunately this selfish practice is now against the law anyway, but if you are interested in helping nature then the last thing you should be doing is raiding the few rich bits of countryside to stock up your garden. In just thirty or forty years, the primrose has become a rare plant in the wild, and one of the main factors leading to its decline has undoubtedly been thoughtless transplanting.

Primroses are one of the obvious woodland wildflowers to grow. I have a large patch in my mini-woodland, growing in the sandy soil around the log-bank, and they flower their heads off from March through April and on into May. Violets are happy in the same habitat, and I have a few oxlip plants amongst mine because the yellow and purple flowers go so well together. Other low-growing woodland-edge flowers you must include are wood anemone, with its dark green cut-leaves and pure white flowers, and the wild strawberry, which scrambles about, rooting down all over the place. Its pretty white flowers are followed by delicious miniature strawberries in July and August. If you have plenty of space, you may be brave enough to plant wild garlic – ramsons. This has a very beautiful white flower in early spring, and the leaves are delicious in salads, but it seeds like mad and does give off rather an overpowering smell of onions, particularly if it gets crushed. Another invasive woodland wildflower which is common enough in gardens but very rare in the countryside is lily of the valley. This is one of the few flowers that will grow really well in the driest of soils, so if you have a big tree casting heavy shade and stealing all the soil moisture, lily of the valley is just the thing to fill that space. The leaves are a very attractive green and the perfume from the spring flowers can be overpowering on a still evening in May or June.

The poplar hawkmoth lays its eggs on the leaves of goat willow (*Salix caprea*) and poplar. Here the big juicy caterpillar is well camouflaged against this underside of a sallow leaf.

The primrose (*Primula vulgaris*) has become quite rare in the countryside. Never dig up wild plants for your garden. Buy them from a nursery, swap them with other wildlife gardening friends, or grow them yourself from seed.

LEFT: The foxglove (*Digitalis purpurea*) is an easy wildflower to grow. Each plant only blooms once, usually in its second year, so you must let some of the seed ripen and germinate, to make sure you have a springtime display year after year.

WILDFLOWERS FOR THE WOODLAND-EDGE HABITAT

Wood anemone (*Anemone nemorosa*) Pretty white 'wind' flowers.

Lords and Ladies (*Arum maculatum*) A whole range of folk-names. Dramatic at every stage of growth, from black-blotched fresh green leaves in spring, through the flowering stage, with its weird, creamy hoodlike flower, to the clusters of bright orange berries.

Greater celandine (*Chelidonium majus*) Yellow sap stains fingers (and anything else it touches). The leaves and flowers are very pretty.

Foxglove (*Digitalis purpurea*) Up to two metres tall. Grows as a biennial, so new seed must be allowed to germinate each year, to provide flowers the year after. May/June is the best time for flowering.

Bluebell (*Endymion non-scriptus*) Spreads quite well once established. You can buy bulbs from specialist nurseries, but beware of pink garden varieties and the much coarser Spanish species. Nothing could be more beautiful than our own, increasingly rare, native bluebell.

Snowdrop (*Galanthus nivalis*) Probably not a true native but so easy to grow that it really is a must. Transplant plants in leaf if you can get them. Otherwise bulbs are readily available, but they can take a season or two to settle down.

Herb robert (*Geranium robertianum*) A colourful little cranesbill with red stems and small pink flowers.

Wood cranesbill (*Geranium sylvaticum*) Much more lush than herb robert, with larger purple flowers.

White deadnettle (*Lamium album*) A super groundcover for the woodland edge. It flowers in spring and autumn most years, and is a marvellous bee-plant.

Yellow archangel (*Lamiastrum galeobdolon*) Much more open habit than the deadnettles, with a rich golden flower colour. An indicator of ancient woodland in the wild.

Red deadnettle (*Lamium purpureum*) Not so tall as its white relative, but with more colourful leaves and a capacity for carpeting shady ground and flowering for six or seven months of the year.

Wild daffodil (*Narcissus pseudo-narcissus*) Still thriving in a few lucky corners of England and Wales. Never dig them up from the countryside. Bulbs are available from specialist nurseries, and that is the way to grow them.

Primrose (*Primula vulgaris*) Easily swamped by taller vegetation. Grow without too much difficulty from seed, and they really do make the woodland-edge complete.

Lesser celandine (*Ranunculus ficaria*) Very invasive, but beautiful nevertheless. Prefers moist ground.

Red campion (*Silene dioica*) Seeds happily into rich soils in dappled shade. Tones perfectly with foxgloves, and flowers a second time in late summer.

Solomon's seal (*Polygonatum multiflorum*) Quite an unusual wildflower, with arching stems of small white flowers and blue-green leaves.

Lily of the valley (*Convallaria majalis*) Grows like mad in some gardens, and proves impossible in others. Very drought-tolerant, with a wonderful fragrance from the white flowers in spring. Look out for the red berries in late summer, too. This plant dies down completely in the autumn, but is easily transplanted. Rare in the wild.

continued on page 53

Common violet (*Viola riviniana*) An important butterfly food-plant, and a lovely addition to the spring garden.

Sweet woodruff (*Galium odoratum*) Whorls of pretty little white flowers on long, thin stems. Can be grown as a tight carpet or allowed to sprawl over other woodland wildflowers.

Stinking hellebore (*Helleborus foetidus*) Dark green leaves the year round. A handsome plant, growing up to 600mm tall, and producing green flowers in early spring.

Stinking iris (*Iris foetidissima*) The flowers are a rather insipid browny-yellow, but beautifully marked. The evergreen strap-like leaves are very useful through the winter, but the star-feature is the fruits. Heavy seedpods split in late summer to reveal neat rows of dazzling orange berry-like seeds.

Wild strawberry (*Fragaria vesca*) A low growing, wiry little plant with white flowers in late spring, and miniature strawberries in late summer. The fruits are delicious, but you need an awful lot to fill a bowl, and the blackbirds and squirrels usually get there first.

Hedge woundwort (*Stachys sylvatica*) Tall, handsome flower spikes, followed by shiny little black seeds in clusters of four.

Garlic mustard (*Alliaria petiolata*) A pretty spring flower with a deep root-stock. It grows as a biennial, and is an important food plant for orange-tip butterflies.

Ramsons (*Allium ursinum*) Introduce this wild garlic at your peril. It is *very* invasive – spreading by both seed and bulb-division. The white flowers are very striking. The leaves are handsome, and even the oniony smell is rather pleasant in small doses.

Nettle-leaved bell-flower (*Campanula trachelium*) Tall, handsome flower with unusual leaves. Very pretty blue.

Green alkanet (*Pentaglottis sempervirens*) A piercing blue flower this time, but the plant is rather coarse and it can be very untidy. Cut back after flowering and you may get a second performance if you're lucky.

Of the taller woodland wildflowers, foxgloves are a must. It is well worth collecting a little seed from wild plants, rather than planting the slightly different garden hybrids. There really is nothing to beat the elegant beauty of those large pink bells with the chocolate brown spots inside, and I sit for hours in spring watching huge bumblebees visiting each pollen store in turn. Remember that foxgloves are biennials. Once a plant has flowered it dies, and seedlings take two years to reach maturity, so you need to sow seed for two consecutive years if you want to establish a colony which will produce flowers annually. There is another wonderful wildflower which is almost the same shade of deep pink, and begins flowering a little earlier than the foxgloves. Pink campion is one of my favourite woodland-edge plants. It grows up to about 600mm tall, flowers off and on from March to October, with its major display very early in the spring, and it produces a carpet of seedlings wherever there is a gap it can reach. Its close relation white campion is just as beautiful, but tends to need more light and often grows as an annual in cultivated but weedy cornfields. Greater celandine is about the same height as the campions, but has lime-green leaves and a wonderful little yellow flower. It is actually much more closely related to the Welsh poppy than the familiar lesser celandine, and if you break off a leaf or an unripe seedpod, you will find that the plant contains a deep yellow sap which will stain your fingers, and was used by our ancestors as a dye for wool.

There are many more woodland wild flowers to choose from, of course – bluebells and Solomon's seal, sweet-smelling woodruff and perhaps the best of all the ground carpeting bumblebee plants, white and red deadnettle – but few if any of these plants will find their way naturally into your new habitat. Woodland plants don't tend to produce mobile seed in the way wasteland plants do. That's why they are so easily lost forever when a wood is destroyed. All of the wildflowers I have mentioned so far are available commercially as seed, and I suggest you begin by growing and planting easy ones like deadnettle and primrose, and as the woodland-edge habitat develops you can add in the plants like wood anemone which are a bit more difficult to get going.

Finally, there are a few plants which make their living by growing up through several layers of this habitat. These are the woodland climbers. You need to wait until your trees and shrubs are strongly established, otherwise they could be overwhelmed, but once you have a sturdy structure emerging it is well worth planting honeysuckle, and possibly the more vigorous wild clematis or old man's beard. There are herbaceous climbers too, such as white bryony, with its fascinating double-spiral tendrils, its bee-busy white-green flowers and its strings of orange, yellow and red poisonous fruit; woody nightshade, with its bunches of wonderful blue-purple and yellow flowers in summer and its equally colourful but slightly less poisonous berries in autumn; and large bell bindweed, whose beautiful white flowers draw such compliments from garden visitors, but whose twining stems can swamp the whole garden in no time at all. Each of these plants has its place of course. I love to see the way bryony can grow from nothing to twenty feet in a summer, and I encourage it to crawl across my inherited golden conifers, but as with so many of our wild plants, they can get out of hand very quickly, and they provide a timely reminder that, although wildlife gardening may mean working much more closely with nature, it is still gardening. My artificial woodland-edge habitat really is very artificial, and there is no point pretending that the rich habitat garden is a particularly easy garden to look after. What I *can* say is that for the gardening work you put in, you will reap far, far more rewards, and certainly your effort will be appreciated by a huge number of grateful wild plants and animals, many of which are too small for you ever to see.

Chapter 5

Hedgerows and climber~ covered screens

THE ASPECT of wildlife habitat destruction that has received most publicity in recent years is the loss of farm hedgerows. Although some of the tens of thousands of miles which have been grubbed out were very old – Saxon boundaries dating back a thousand years for instance – most of the hedges were relatively modern in landscape terms. The enclosure which carved up the common land and led to so much hedge-planting mainly took place between 150 and 200 years ago. These hedgerows were much more modern than, say, the ancient woodlands, but they were extremely important for wildlife. Because they were planted in the Arcadian days before intensive farming, when there were wildflowers and butterflies everywhere, the 'new' hedgerows were able to inherit an extremely rich woodland overspill. The wildflowers and less mobile invertebrates of the deepest woodland were unable to move out and occupy this new eighteenth century habitat boom, but many of the more mobile species did take up residence, and as the original woodlands were then destroyed, the field hedgerows became more and more important as a mini-habitat for refugee woodlanders.

The other, perhaps more significant contribution which hedgerows made to wildlife in the farming countryside, was to provide a green, sheltered, relatively safe corridor system for animals and plants to move along. As the arable fields and pastures were made more hostile to wildlife, the hedgerows became the only relatively pollution-free means of travelling from one sanctuary to another. Now many of the hedgerows have gone. They are simply not compatible with the scale of modern mechanical farming. With heavy machinery and a grant to cover the costs, it has been all too easy to remove even the most critical of ancient landscape features without a second thought.

In the wildlife garden, a good mixed country hedgerow can provide a marvellous scaled-down version of the woodland edge, in much the same

Country-style hedgerows don't have to be overgrown and tangled. This neatly clipped boundary of fieldmaple (*Acer campestre*) is still a marvellous addition to the rich-habitat garden.

way as it did two hundred years ago in the countryside. You get a lot of habitat in very little space, and if enough of your neighbours plant or conserve hedges, then you will set up a good ecological corridor system which will shelter hedgehogs, weasels, mice and small birds as they roam around from garden to garden.

Modern garden hedges are good nesting habitat. The mere act of clipping produces a dense, twiggy cover, and no matter how alien the plant species, birds such as the thrush, the blackbird and the dunnock will happily build there. As you will have gathered from all my talk of 'native species' in the chapter on woodland edge, though, there is more to habitat creation than just providing physical support for birds nests. The same principles apply here. There is a whole range of vigorous native shrubs which have been used for generations as hedgerow plants in the countryside. In fact a hedge is perhaps the best way of all to provide a comprehensive range of native leaves and soft, juicy shoots for the caterpillars and grubs of all those native invertebrates. Even forest tree species can be kept at a manageable size by clipping as a hedge, and although some dependent insects seem to need their oak or beech leaves to be blowing in the wind 30 metres above ground, many are just as happy munching away in a hedge as they would be in a forest-size tree. It is possible to grow quite a range of woodland-edge wildflowers along a hedge-bottom, too. Some of them do need shade, and will do best on the side away from the sun, and many of them have problems if the ground becomes very dry, but given a reasonable soil, and perhaps a bit of extra water in very dry weather, you should be able to grow a smashing, colourful ribbon of wildflowers along the strip immediately in front of the hedge. Woodland-edge species such as foxglove, campion, primrose, greater celandine and violet will all thrive, and several other species actually seem to grow better here. Where there is shelter but lots of light, hedge woundwort is a marvellous plant, with tall spikes of brownish purple flowers. This is very much a 'bee' plant, but the lipped flowers are not very big, and so the relatively small species of bee find it particularly attractive. I grow it through a carpet of more prostrate white and red deadnettle, and in early spring the whole hedge bottom really does buzz with activity. The detail of many of these wildflowers is exquisite, and a feature of hedge woundwort which I love is the way the seeds are packaged. Look deep into the old flower socket when the blossom has fallen, and you will see a neat cluster of three or four tiny shiny black seeds peeping out at you.

Cuckoo-pint is another dramatic hedge-bottom wildflower, exciting at every stage of its development. The blotched leaves are a remarkable rich, deep green when they burst through and unfold in early spring. The flower structure is spectacular – a subtle, soft green colour for the delicate-looking hoodlike spathe or sheath, and in the centre, the rather phallic spadix. This gives off a faint smell of unpleasant decay which seems irresistible to flies. Once pollinated, the sheath withers and a column of fresh green berries develops. These berries turn brilliant vermilion orange in the late summer, and really brighten up the hedgerow, though the berries are very poisonous. Another common name for cuckoo-pint is Lords and Ladies, and there are any number of erotic theories about the origins of that name.

One more hedge-bottom wildflower that is worth finding a place for is garlic mustard. This common white flower, with its fresh green leaves, tinged with purple, has nothing whatever to do with garlic, but if you crush the leaves there is a faint oniony smell. The other common name you sometimes hear is Jack-by-the-hedge. This plant flowers early in the year, and is an important food source for overwintering butterflies as they emerge from hibernation. It is also one of the three or four types of plant which orange-tip butterflies lay their eggs on, and for that reason alone there should always be a place for it in our wildlife gardens.

The hedge bottom is the traditional place to throw rubbish. Pull into any rural lay-by and I'm afraid you will see all too clearly what I mean. I'm certainly not advocating a wildlife habitat made up of old mattresses and bicycle frames, however good that may be for certain species, but I do think it is a good idea to let garden rubbish build up along the hedge bottom. When you sweep the autumn leaves from the lawn, or chop down the spent raspberry canes at the end of the summer, don't burn them. Put them under the hedge as an organic mulch. There they will provide food for a whole mass of mini-beasts, and could even be the spot your local hedgehog chooses for hibernating.

I do hope you will find somewhere to plant a hedge. I have replaced about fifty metres of rickety wooden fence with new hedgerow planting, and used another hedge to screen off the vegetable patch. It was cheap and easy to do, and already, after only a couple of years, I can see that lots of wildlife has moved in and colonised the new slimline habitat. There really is a big choice of species you can use but if you want my specific suggestion, then why not plant a mixture of 75% hawthorn, to give you a thorny, dense hedge which blackbirds and finches will nest in, 15% field maple, a shrub with a similar shaped leaf to hawthorn, but with lovely soft brown shades in the spring regrowth, and no thorns, and then 2% each of holly and native wild privet, for a splash of evergreen winter leaf colour, dogwood for the red colour of its stems, guelder rose and dog rose. Plant two-year-old seedlings, which are readily available from any good nursery, and I suggest you use about five plants for each metre of hedge. I find it helps establishment if I plant the seedlings so that they all slope along the line of the hedge in the same direction at about 45°.

If I cut off the side shoots and about one third off the top of each plant, then by the end of the first summer the hedge is already pretty dense at the

THIS PAGE: If you can afford the space, do let your hedge grow a little bit wild. Hawthorn is so much more valuable if it can flower and fruit. This tapestry of old man's beard and wild rose really conjours up the spirit of autumn.

OPPOSITE: Elder is another valuable hedgerow shrub. The dazzling white flowers are marvellous for insects in spring; and a whole variety of garden birds will gorge themselves on the elderberries in late summer.

base. My mixed field hedge was also helped by mulching with two parallel strips of a material very much like roofing felt, which is manufactured specially for the job.

Of course if you don't fancy this kind of mixed hedge, though I must say I do love the way all the difference leaf shapes blend together into a kind of living tapestry, then you can always plant a single species hedge. Any of the species in the mixture will do, or there are colourful alternatives like beech, or more sombre native shrubs such as yew or box.

Whatever you choose to plant, do try and experiment a little, particularly when it comes to clipping. If you get it right, with just one cut a year in early summer, you can get quite a neat hawthorn hedge to cover itself with May blossom. A cut at the end of winter will provide you with plenty of regrowth in the dogwood to give you red stem-colour right through to the following spring. Don't forget, though, that for maximum wildlife value the hedge does need to produce some soft, chewable leaves and shoots, and please remember *never* to cut the hedge during the nesting season. You may not physically damage the nest, but the disturbance and the dramatic change to the look of the surroundings almost always leads to the parent birds deserting, and that is the last thing you want to happen.

I promised at the beginning of this book that you could attract wildlife into even the tiniest of town gardens. So far I've talked about nothing but mini-woodlands and country hedgerows, and obviously if you look out on little more than a light-well then I won't have helped you much. Your salvation comes with climbers. In the wild there are several plants that scramble and twine their way up bushes and tree trunks, or cascade down cliff faces. None of them are particularly choosy about what they use for support, and if you have any kind of reasonably solid, vertical surface you should be trying to cover it with plants.

Of all the climbing plants you could possibly grow, there is no doubt in my mind about which is the best for wildlife. Ivy. No wonder the ancient Brits thought it had magical properties. First of all, it is really very easy to grow. It likes shade best, and a reasonably rich soil, but in fact it will grow pretty well anywhere. It grows up vertical surfaces without any need for wires or bits of string, though it sometimes needs some encouragement at first. If you buy a plant in a pot, it will probably be tied to a cane and looking rather forlorn. Plant it at least 300mm away from the bottom of the wall or fence, so that its roots aren't in the very hostile drought zone. That is good policy whichever climbers you choose. Then summon up all your courage, forget about how much you've just shelled out for the cane, and chop the plant down to 100mm or so above the ground. What that apparently brutal act of vandalism does is give a boost to the roots and stimulate the production of vigorous young side-shoots with instant sticking power. If the ivy is planted on the sunny side of the

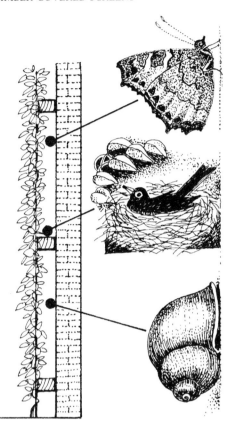

Train your climbing plants a few centimetres away from walls and fences. The shady space that this creates will be popular with hibernating butterflies, nesting birds and garden snails.

wall, then it seems to help in the first few months of growth if you shade the plant. Just lean a piece of wood or a sheet of corrugated iron against the wall so that it leaves the young plant in a shadow. It is important that you water climbers in the early stages, too. It can get very dry at the bottom of a wall. The foundations tend to absorb soil moisture and make the problem particularly bad.

The great thing about ivy as a wildlife climber is the variety of ways in which it supports wild creatures. Being evergreen it provides very good cover throughout the year, of course, and an ivy-covered wall is a favourite nesting site for wrens. Blackbirds often build in older ivy, too. Ivy is particularly important as wildlife cover in the winter, with several species of butterfly hibernating amongst its leaves. The brimstone, for instance, often the last butterfly to be seen around in the autumn, and a real harbinger of the following spring, seems perfectly camouflaged for overwintering amongst the ivy. When it flies, its wings are a wonderful soft lemon yellow, but when it settles, and its wings close, the colour and pattern are exactly like those of a dead ivy leaf. When it hangs itself up for the winter it simply disappears.

In my garden there is ivy growing tightly over a low brick wall by the back door. In the daytime it looks innocent enough, but if I take a torch out, particularly on a damp, warm night, there are dozens and dozens of snails gliding around the wall and the surrounding paths. Obviously the deep, cool shade of the ivy foliage is just what snails like to keep them safe during the heat of the day.

Ivy doesn't stop at simple physical protection either. Its flowers last longer into the winter than almost any other British plant, often carrying golden blobs of sweet life-giving nectar right through into December. It only flowers once it reaches maturity, and it seems to need to climb up to at least a metre or so too, but once it starts, an arborescent flowering ivy will pull in late autumn insects from the whole neighbourhood. I watched a bank of really good ivy flowers in a park one October and estimated that there was an average of seven fabulous small tortoiseshell butterflies to the square metre, all gently sipping away at the nectar to the point of intoxication. The flowers on my own ivy attract a marvellous variety of hoverflies in October and November, and really do provide a focus for insect-watching at that time of year.

After the flower comes the fruit, and again the ivy is terrific. Most years the clusters of berry-like fruits are only ripening to their mature purple/black stage at the end of the winter, when most other natural food such as hips and haws has been eaten up. Redwings and fieldfares often gorge themselves on ivy fruits before leaving for the long journey back north to their breeding sites, and last spring a couple of comical, very

The hedge-bottom is a very special habitat. Lords and ladies, or cuckoo-pint (*Arum maculatum*) is just one of the fascinating native plants that grow here.

portly wood pigeons entertained us for hours, trying to balance on the thin twigs at the top of the elm hedge, whilst they reached out desperately to grab at the ivy crop.

People worry terribly about the effect on their buildings of climbers such as ivy. All sorts of stories circulate about demolished masonry. The fact is that climbers are much more likely to *protect* your brickwork, insulating it from the effects of frost and direct sunshine. Problems only seem to arise if the wall is already on its last legs, and even then, ivy is only likely speed up the problem if the wall is old enough to have been built with relatively soft lime mortar, instead of the less hospitable modern cement.

If you are worried about all those self-clinging aerial roots bringing the house down, then it is simple enough to grow a climber which doesn't cling directly to the wall. In fact, apart from the climbing hydrangea and Virginia creeper, most garden climbers need a wire or a pole to cling to. Wildlife will make most use of the gap between the outer leaves and the wall or fence, and for this reason it is worth manipulating this habitat a little. Normally you would expect to fix your climbing wires an inch or two from the wall. Traditionally, gardeners have used flat nails with a hole in, known as vine-eyes, to hold the wires a little away from the surface. What I suggest is that you strain your climber support at least 100mm away from the wall. You can do this easily, either by making use

Our own native honeysuckle (*Lonicera periclymenum*) is a lovely climber to grow. Its perfume fills the June garden and attracts many of the more spectacular moths. Its colourful berries help feed the birds in autumn.

of any brick piers or projecting fence posts that already exist; fixing 100mm square blocks to the wall and stretching wires between their outer faces, or driving in special new posts a little way out from the wall and effectively erecting a wire fence between them. Fit in a few simple wooden ledges and platforms between the wall or fence and your climber framework, and then train your climber up to form an outer screen. You will be delighted by the amount of wildlife activity that takes place on the other side of the green curtain. Birds will nest there, butterflies will hibernate and you may even accommodate a bat roost if you are really lucky.

Of the non-clinging native climbers you can choose from, honeysuckle probably gives the best value. It climbs by twining its stems around the support, and may need a bit of tying in at first, till it gets the idea. There is no more dreamy perfume on a June evening, and by growing it against a wall you can bury your nose right in amongst the blossoms. Honeysuckle is one of the classic moth flowers, and it can be particularly successful if you train it up a wall with an outside light on it. You can look forward to the sight of large hawkmoths bobbing meticulously from flower to flower, hovering at the entrance and then probing deep inside and sucking up the nectar. If the perfume doesn't captivate them, then the lamplight will generally do the trick. Insist on the native honeysuckle, rather than some garden hybrid, and then you will be sure of a good crop of scarlet berries to follow the flowers. The young shoots are often attacked by blackfly too, and from now on you can view this as an asset, since the aphids will quickly be followed by ladybirds and lacewings, and the larvae of such insects as the spectacular, but quite harmless scorpion fly. Where would the wildlife gardener be without aphids?

Even the bark of honeysuckle has its uses, believe it or not. On an old plant, the bark tends to strip off in long, tough, stringy lumps, a bit like short lengths of raffia. This makes marvellous nest-building material, and in early spring you will see everything from house sparrows to blackbirds tugging strips off. In ancient oak woodland, where honeysuckle grows naturally, one species of rare bird, the pied flycatcher, depends almost entirely on honeysuckle bark for nest-building. With coppice woodlands being neglected, honeysuckle dies out and the visiting pied flycatchers become rarer and rarer.

One more native climber deserves special mention. In fact this time it is normally more of a scrambler. How about growing a bramble up your wall? It will mean quite a lot of work if you are to keep it under control, but there really are few plants more beautiful, and for wildlife the blackberry bush is a winner. It's very easy to grow from a cutting or a layering, and since brambles vary enormously in the wild I suggest you choose a parent plant which has proved to be a heavy, sweet fruiter, and propagate your garden plant from that. Train it on wires, and prune it the way you would a cultivated loganberry, on a two-year rotation, cutting out the old canes after their second season, once they have fruited. In the prize fruit garden you would probably remove the old stems from the base in early autumn, but in the wildlife garden I suggest you leave these on until the spring. That way you will provide maximum shelter each winter. The bramble is a native plant which supports a great many dependent insects. A quick glance at the old leaves will show you how many little creatures have given them a bite or at least a nasty suck. The beautiful blossoms are a particularly good source of pollen, and popular with bees, and they also attract the late spring butterflies. Gatekeeper or hedgebrown, speckled wood, peacock, small tortoiseshell and comma all feed on the bramble flowers in my garden. From mid-August onwards there will be colourful bunches of blackberries for you and the wildlife to enjoy. Masses of them hang over the garden wall outside my window, and each year the crown fruits at the tip of each bunch seem to ripen just in time for the mother blackbird to pluck each one, and feed it to one or other of her enormous, impatient offspring. There is lots of colour in the leaves and stems of the bramble, too, and in a sheltered spot, particularly when it is trained as a wall plant, you can expect the handsome five-part leaves to turn all shades of crimson, copper and gold, and to cling on right until the last frost of spring. Often the new side shoots are several inches long before the old leaves fall, so it is virtually evergreen.

There isn't a lot to choose between the exotic climbers and wall shrubs you can grow. Some of the honeysuckles have as rich a perfume and nectar supply as our own native species. Several of the species clematis produce even fluffier seedheads than our own wild old man's beard. Shrubs like ceanothus and cotoneaster are first class pollen plants, and pyracantha is famous for its autumn berries. All of them will give you the wildlife shelter you're looking for, and of course they wouldn't be in popular cultivation if they weren't beautiful things to look at.

There is one final category of climbers that is well worth mentioning, and that is the annuals. When you think about it, there are really quite a lot of climbing, twining plants you can grow from seed, and they are very useful, particularly in the early years when you are waiting for the more permanent perennials to become established. You may have to change your ideas a bit, but how about growing a curtain of runner beans up your wildlife garden wall? You will be able to watch bees squeezing their way into the bright red flowers all summer long, and have the added bonus of a crop at the end of it. If you watch carefully you will probably observe some of the insect pollinators 'beating the system'. Instead of struggling to open the jaws of the bean flowers, quite a few of the bees have developed the trick of biting a small hole in the base of the flower, and pinching the nectar without ever fulfilling their part of the bargain by pollinating the plant. Even if you don't actually see the cheats in action, you will be able to find plenty of the little holes they have left behind. Runner beans have scarlet flowers, but I must admit I stopped growing them years ago. I found the beans were stringy almost before they were big enough to eat. I now grow climbing French beans instead. The flavour is every bit as good, the plants don't grow quite so enormous, and there is a choice of blue beans as well as green. Flowers vary in colour from cream to purple.

Nasturtiums are well worth a place in the wildlife garden, too. Choose a vigorous climbing strain, preferably with a perfume, plant in poor soil for maximum flower colour, and stand well back. Once they get going, these annual climbers grow at an amazing pace. The flowers are popular with bees, and quite a range of small pollinating beetles, too. The seeds are presumably eaten by small mammals in the winter, and the leaves are an alternative food source for caterpillars of the cabbage white butterfly. It would be nice to think that, if you grew nasturtiums, the caterpillars would leave your cabbages alone, but I'm afraid the more probable outcome is simply an extra supply of egg-laying females the following year. Cabbage white caterpillars aren't the only things that enjoy eating nasturtium leaves, of course. They are a favourite with aphids too. Several other kinds of caterpillar seem to like them, and I'm rather partial to them myself. They add a lovely sharp, peppery zing to summer salads. One of the great flavours of childhood, too, comes with that moment when you bite the pointed tip off the back end of your first nasturtium 'hat' and suck out the sugary nectar. The bean-flower robbing bees don't have all the tricks!

Next spring, when you are stocking up with seed packets, and pretending to yourself that this year they really will get planted, look out for annual climbers. There are ornamental gourds with huge yellow flowers, the cup and saucer vine (*Cobaea scandens*), with wonderful purple bell flowers; canary creeper, 'love in a puff' and quite a few more. Start them off in a pot on the kitchen windowsill, train them up your climber support and you could have an irresistibly picturesque setting for your spotted fly-catcher nest by the end of May.

Chapter 6

Live~in lawns
and wildflower meadows

IF YOU close your eyes and drift off into your ideal, imaginary
landscape, I guarantee that within minutes you will be climbing over a
stile or squeezing through a kissing gate – into a sunny, wildflower
meadow. All those Monet and Renoir prints on Boots staircase, and the
pictures in our earliest school reading books have helped build up this
romantic image of the countryside. Things are rather different when you
set off in search of your dream landscape, and meet up with the harsh
reality of wall-to-wall sugar beet, zero grazing and green deserts of
ryegrass. Wildflower meadows are almost entirely a thing of the past.
You may still see the odd field of buttercups or dandelions, and the
County Naturalists Trusts have managed to buy up one or two of the
very best examples of truly ancient meadow, but the statistics show quite
clearly that we are now left with less than 5% of all the unimproved
pasture that still existed as recently as 1949. We must have half a million
acres of regularly mown lawns in our suburban gardens, and at least as
much again in our urban parks. It seems such a shame to adopt the high
technology of chemical agriculture here, when we could be providing a
valuable habitat for all those refugee cowslips with nowhere to go.

Certainly it is possible to conserve a great many of our meadow
wildflowers in wildlife gardens. It is also possible, if enough people take
the plunge, to reverse the falling trend in the population of many of our
grassland insect species, too. In the very first year of meadow management on my old lawn I had meadow brown and common blue butterflies
breeding – and the whole thing is less than ten metres across. I know there
must be small mammals in there too, because the local kestrel drops in
from time to time, and, rather less pleasingly, next-door's cat has a field
day. I suspect we are unlikely to see skylarks nesting in gardens. The cats
would certainly make their life difficult, and probably they need a
minimum size of meadow, but I am quite convinced that if we could

persuade the local authorities to bring back wildflower meadows to our parks and public open spaces, we could have lots of skylarks in the heart of town, and even corncrakes would return. Their near extinction is particularly sad because they actually fly from Africa to Britain each summer to breed. We are very self-satisfied about our conservation conscience compared with that of the third world, yet we have destroyed their breeding habitat to such an extent that within less than forty years they have been driven to the furthest corners of their territory. The few that still survive fly all the way over the barren lands of Britain's productive farmland, and if they are lucky they find a pocket of flowery, 'unimproved' meadow in the Outer Hebrides or the west of Ireland. They won't be safe there for long either, as vast sums of public money are used to drain land and pour on chemicals in a desperate effort to bring crofters into the agricultural surpluses jamboree. Wouldn't it be marvellous if migrant corncrakes were able to drop with a croak of relief into one of your dream meadows in Birmingham, or Manchester or Glasgow? Start the ball rolling with your 'pocket handkerchief' and I'm sure it will happen in the parks.

All our rich grassland wildlife was developed as a happy spin-off from

WILDFLOWERS FOR THE SPRING MEADOW

(mow from July onwards)

Milkmaids or Lady's smock (*Cardamine pratensis*) Pink flower. 300mm tall. Food-plant of the orange-tip butterfly.

Cowslip (*Primula veris*) Clusters of yellow flowers. Prefers slightly limy soil.

Snakehead fritillary (*Fritillaria meleagris*) Plant as corms. Very beautiful purple-chequered or white flowers. Prefer moist, non-acid soils.

Lesser stitchwort (*Stellaria graminea*) Present in many old lawns. Sprinkles the grasses with tiny white flowers.

Self-heal (*Prunella vulgaris*) A tough little creeping plant with blue/purple flowers.

Bugle (*Ajuga reptans*) Similar to self-heal, but taller spikes of blue flowers and a preference for damp conditions.

Daisy (*Bellis perennis*) What can I say?

Cat's ear (*Hypochoeris radicata*) A very common rosette-weed of poor lawns. Lovely yellow flowers on 300mm stems.

Rough hawkbit (*Leontodon hispidus*) Similar to cat's-ear, but less wiry and much taller.

Dandelion (*Taraxacum officinale*) A sign of deep, rich soil. Quite a useful butterfly nectar plant, and bullfinches love pulling the 'clocks' to pieces and eating the seed.

Yellow rattle (*Rhinanthus minor*) A modest little plant, semi-parasitic on grasses, and producing large (10mm diameter) seed-pods in which the seeds rattle.

Salad burnet (*Sanguisorba minor*) Purple flower over attractive foliage. Prefers moist soil, and the leaves taste like walnut-oil (if you have a vivid imagination). Nice addition to cheese sandwiches.

traditional farming of one sort or another. It was the regular, methodical, annual cycle of mowing and grazing which provided the ideal conditions for all those wildflowers, butterflies and birds we miss so much. It is a change in this pattern which has led to their decline. The success of the wildflower meadow in your garden will depend basically on your willingness to adopt a particular pattern of mowing, and stick to it. You can see how true this is if you look at any normal garden lawn. Presumably it will have been mown on the same steady cycle of a cut every Sunday for summer after summer. That particular pattern favours some of the lawn grasses, which is why we do it, but it also provides a suitable habitat for several species of wildflower. These are generally the species that can live for years without the need to flower, and which hold their leaves very close to the ground. We call them lawn weeds, and everyone is familiar with them. The most common ones are daisies, plantains and catsear, all with the same growth pattern of a flat rosette of leaves. There are creeping plants too, that sneak about below the mower blades, and the commonest of these are selfheal and speedwell. These are the wildflowers best suited to a 'formal lawn' pattern of mowing regime, and if you want to keep them you must stick to the usual timetable, and keep dragging the mower out each week. You can give yourself a treat each year, though. Some time around the middle to the end of May, take a couple of Sundays off. After just a few days of 'neglect', flower stems will rise up from the centre of each of your rosette lawn weeds. Catsear will give you sheets of yellow, daisies will mingle with the bright blue carpet of speedwell, and plantain will surprise you with the beauty of its pollen-covered stamens. You can repeat this lawn-weed wildflower exhibition year after year, but you must return to close mowing again within a month or so, otherwise the lawn grasses will grow up, over-shadow the leaves of the rosette plants, and your daisies and plantain will wither away.

You may decide you would like to change your style of management completely for part of your lawn. I really wanted a meadow at the far end of my garden, beyond the pond, and was keen to leave the lawn uncut until high summer, so that the grasses would get a chance to flower. It was easy enough to do. I simply avoided mowing the new 'meadow' area until the grasses had flowered. Within a couple of seasons, as I expected, all the daisies had gone, but I had a pleasant surprise, too. Some of the plants which had been growing in a suppressed form amongst the close-mown grasses grew up, flowered *and* survived the competition of the taller vegetation. The most successful of these is yarrow, which is present in most people's lawn as a tight, fern-like, emerald-green carpet. It now graces my meadow with its plates of nectar-rich white flowers from mid-July to September, and its leaves have grown up among the grasses. There were a few other meadow flowers lying incognito in my lawn too.

OVERLEAF: One of the secrets is to keep the more orthodox close-mown lawns and grasspaths looking really neat and tidy. That way everyone can see that the uncut meadow isn't just the bit you forgot to mow.

One of the prettiest was lesser stitchwort, and its clouds of bright white flowers are sprinkled everywhere throughout the spring meadow. I had sheets of milkmaids, or lady's smock – the cuckoo flower – growing there. They can't have had a chance to flower for years, and yet as soon as I stopped mowing, up came all these beautiful pink flowers, and down came the orange-tip butterflies to feed on the nectar, and lay eggs on the leaves.

I was particularly fortunate with my lawn. It was old, and weedy, and the soil beneath it is very poor indeed – almost pure sand in fact. This low fertility is very important. If you have rich, deep soil then the grasses do really well, particularly tall, coarse species like cock's foot, and the only wildflower that is likely to survive the competition is cow parsley. You can use your lawnmower to lower the soil fertility, and that may be the best policy for the first couple of years. Keep mowing closely, but make sure you take off the clippings each time, and resist all temptation to add any fertilizer. Each time you cart away a bag of clippings you are taking out a little more of the fertility, the coarse plants will do less and less well, and you will improve your wildflowers' chances. Mix the mowings in with the compost heap, or add them as a mulch to the vegetable garden where the fertility will be a positive advantage.

If your garden is big enough, you might like to develop two or three slightly different meadow communities. Perhaps the area nearest the

WILDFLOWERS FOR THE SUMMER MEADOW

(mow till June and again late September)

Knapweed (*Centaurea scabiosa*) A tough plant with dark, hairy stems and a thistle-like purple flower. Important nectar plant in late summer.

Lady's bedstraw (*Galium verum*) Masses of tiny little bright-yellow flowers, sprawling around in clusters amongst the grass-stems. A food-plant for some of the more spectacular moth caterpillars, and once widely used as a dried 'strewing herb' to cover the floor and disguise the smells of medieval living.

Sheep's sorrel (*Rumex acetosella*) Lends a lovely orange haze to the summer meadow. The seed is an important food for finches, and the leaves are used for egg-laying by the small copper butterfly. An indicator of slightly acid soils.

Field scabious (*Knautia arvensis*) One of the prettiest of our meadow wildflowers. 'Pincushions' of mauve-blue flowers. Very popular with beetles and moths as a source of nectar and pollen.

Ox-eye daisy (*Leucanthemum vulgare*) One of the easiest meadow flowers to grow, though it will tend to die out after four or five years unless the 'meadow' is disturbed a little – perhaps by trampling.

Hardhead (*Centaurea nigra*) Very similar to knapweed.

house will remain close-mown, with that flowery hiccup in June to surprise the neighbours. Obviously close-mown lawns are very useful in a garden. It would be silly to leave yourself with nowhere to sit on sunny days. A second area might be managed specifically for spring wild-flowers. If you mow it regularly after the end of June, this will allow flowers like the lady's smock, fritillary, selfheal, bugle, moonpenny, cowslip, yellow rattle and dandelion to flower and set ripe seed, but will give you a usable lawn for the summer holidays, and will tend to help the spring flowers spread and germinate. Some of our most spectacular wildflower meadows are managed more or less along the same lines. North Meadow, in Oxfordshire, for example, has been mown for hay in early July for generations. The cropped field is rested for a couple of months, and then cattle are put out to graze the aftermath through the late autumn and winter. This pattern has produced the wonderful community of spring meadow flowers. Almost the entire surviving British population of snake-head fritillaries grows here, setting seed in June before the hay is cut. The cattle grazing prevents the swamping of spring flowers by coarse grasses, and also plays an important role in lightly trampling or 'poaching' the ground. Without the cattle churning the surface with their hooves, the wildflower seed would be much less likely to get down through the mat of grasses and germinate.

If you want to simulate the trampling of North Meadow accurately in

Meadow buttercup (*Ranunculus acris*) So much more handsome than the creeping buttercup. The leaves are finely divided and the beautiful single flowers stand up to a metre tall, on elegant, slender, green stems.

Yarrow (*Achillea millefolium*) A lawn weed that spreads like mad – its fern-like leaves are very pretty, and the plates of white flowers are an important source of mid-summer nectar.

Devil's bit scabious (*Succisa pratensis*) Much smaller, darker blue flowers than field scabious, and with no outer 'frill' of ray-flowers. Leaves are the food plant of marsh fritillary butterflies, and this plant will bloom from July until November. Prefers damp conditions.

Musk mallow (*Malva moschata*) A very big meadow plant, growing up to 1.5 metres even in mown conditions.

Well worth growing for its lovely pale pink flowers up to 50mm across.

Harebell (*Campanula rotundifolia*) Can get overwhelmed in all but the poorest of soils, but if you can grow it it gives a real reminder of the countryside.

Perforated St John's Wort (*Hypericum perforatum*) A rapid coloniser, and a useful insect-plant, growing to 300–450mm tall in solid stands. The flowers are yellow and orange.

Goatbeard (*Tragopogon pratensis*) Much more than just 'another dandelion'. The seedheads are huge – real 'grandfather clocks' and they seem to stay in one piece rather longer than ordinary dandelions. They look spectacular in the shallow light of evening.

A century ago there were hundreds of wet pastures just like North Meadow. Now this national nature reserve is almost all that is left of our native population of that most beautiful of meadow wildflowers, the snakehead fritillary (*Fritillaria meleagria*) …

your garden then you need to organise a garden party in late August, where you can ply your livestock with gin and tonic, and then wheel out your mechanical grazing machine, the lawn mower, for an extra couple of cuts at the end of the growing season.

Some of the meadow flowers don't bloom until August or September, and if you adopt the spring-meadow cycle then obviously they will not survive. I'm thinking of the taller species such as field scabious, knapweed, hardhead, meadow clary and musk mallow. To encourage these particular plants you need a third mowing regime, which leaves the meadow uncut until the end of the summer – say mid to late September. You must cut then, of course, and you must take away the hay. If you leave all the cut stems through the winter you will have a very tangled mess by spring, and the only wild flowers that will survive that treatment are nettles and hogweed.

Late-summer meadows really are lovely. All the flower colours seem to be pastel shades of mauve and lilac, and the shallower sunlight at the end of the year produces some very beautiful effects. Quite a few of these taller, late flowering species don't really begin to grow until mid-summer, so if you are short of space you can mow this section of the meadow in the early part of the year, and use it as a rough lawn whilst the cowslips and fritillaries of the spring meadow are out of bounds. Don't cut the grass too close, though, or you will damage the wildflowers and they will gradually disappear. 75mm should be the minimum.

Adopting a different mowing regime will provide the right habitat for meadow wildlife, but apart from a few odd plants like yarrow, you won't have the meadow species there to take up residence. The more mobile animal life will find your new habitat surprisingly quickly, but most of the wildflowers will have to be introduced artificially – just like the primroses and foxgloves of the woodland edge. In the wild, the flower seed is scattered around in the wind, and then pressed into the soil by the cattle, and you can try sprinkling packets of cowslip seed amongst your garden party guests if you like, but even in the cow pasture the success rate is extremely low, and with wildflower seed the price it is, I suggest you adopt a more efficient technique. Plan to introduce a selection of species which will flower to suit the particular mowing regime you have adopted. It is worth checking the type of soil you have, too. You may just happen to have one which is particularly acid or very chalky, extra wet or very, very well drained. If it is extreme in some way, then that will restrict the range of wildflowers you can grow, though it may offer you possibilities that aren't available to wildlife gardeners with more normal, middle of the road kinds of soil.

Once you have made your selection, buy the seed in individual packets, preferably from one of the seedsmen who deal only in native stock. There is quite a difference between subspecies of some of our wildflowers when you compare native flora with their counterparts in France or Holland, for example, and certainly it is better for wildlife generally if we try to avoid introducing foreign seed stock, even into our gardens.

When your seed arrives, rather than sow it straight on to the meadow, where little, if any, of it will germinate successfully, sow it instead in pots or seed trays filled with a normal, sterilised seed compost – John Innes No. 1, for instance. The best time to sow most species is in late summer. If you think about it, this is the natural time of year for seed to reach the soil anyway. Put the pots outside, in a cold corner of the garden, and forget about them. What you shouldn't do is keep the pots inside through the winter. If you do, then some of the species will germinate in December or January, and you will be landed with a mass of seedlings and nowhere to put them. They will be too tender to plant outside. Most of the seed, though, will probably not germinate at all if you keep it inside. A great many of our native wildflowers need a period of really cold weather, with many degrees of frost, before they are in a suitable condition to germinate. It is a strategy which helps them survive in the wild, by preventing early germination in mild mid-winter weather, and then premature death in the frost that follows. By putting your autumn-sown seeds out in the cold you are helping prepare them for effective germination the following spring. Once April comes, make sure the

...but fritillarias, and many other beautiful grassland species, can be grown successfully in gardens – if you just manage your lawn a little differently.

WILDFLOWERS FOR THE 'CULTIVATED CORNFIELD WEED' PATCH

Corncockle (*Agrostemma githago*) Tall and elegant – and now extremely rare in the wild. The big, black seeds are easy to sow, and the mauve flowers stand up to 1 metre tall, and are extremely beautiful.

Scarlet pimpernel (*Anagallis arvensis*) A tiny creeping plant with poppy-red flowers which open in the sun and close at the first sign of rain. Quite a common garden weed.

Corn marigold (*Chrysanthemum segetum*) One of our prettiest wildflowers, and an easy annual to grow. The yellow daisy-like flowers are very colourful.

Red deadnettle (*Lamium purpureum*) Often crops up in the first year after cultivation. The leaves have a purple tinge to them too, and the plant seems able to tolerate the shade of the taller annuals, and creeps around beneath the more colourful weeds.

Pineapple mayweed (*Matricaria matricarioides*) One of those evocative smells of childhood. Squeeze the plump green flower between finger and thumb and smell the pineapple perfume that gives this common weed its name.

Common poppy (*Papaver rhoeas*) A great favourite, and rightly so. The colour really is spectacular, and poppy seedlings will reappear year after year if you simply rake over the surface at the end of each summer. It is no use trying to grow poppies in the meadow, though. They are annuals and must have a disturbed habitat.

Cornflowers (*Centaurea cyanus*) Another of those penetrating blues. Cornflowers must have made our countryside look quite magical when they were common weeds in cornfields. Avoid all those new fancy pinks, mauves and whites if you possibly can. Cornflowers last surprisingly well as cut flowers.

compost is kept moist, and all being well you will have germinating seedlings by the end of the month.

Quite a few species may not germinate the first year, even after frost treatment. Cowslips are one example of a species the seeds of which germinate only if they are very, very fresh (and that can never be the case with packeted seeds) or when they have had two or even three winters of cold weather treatment. It may be frustrating but just be patient. Keep an eye on the pots each spring, and just when you have abandoned all hope, up will come the cowslip seedlings. This is one of the reasons why it is so important to use sterilised compost for seed-growing. It may take cowslips several winters before they germinate, but if you sow them in ordinary soil, dozens of other 'weed' species will germinate at the first sign of spring, and you will never find your cowslips, even if they do manage to come to life. I know a great many people who have bought wildflower seed in the past. If they have chosen an easy species then they have been delighted, and perfectly satisfied. But many of them have gone for difficult seed, like cowslips, and all too often they have thrown the apparently barren compost away, not realising that their precious seeds are just taking their time.

Once your seedlings are big enough to handle, usually at the three or four leaf stage, tease them gently out of the moist compost, and plant them on into individual pots, this time using a slightly richer potting compost, J.I. No. 2. Put them in a sheltered spot where you can keep them watered and watch them grow. I would choose 60 or 75mm plant pots, and leave the seedlings in these for a whole summer. They should grow into good healthy plants, filling the pots with roots and producing lots of leaves. If they start to produce flower shoots, cut these off, and concentrate the plant's energy on growing roots. At the end of the summer, when the 'hay crop' has been cleared and the last tidy-up mowing has been done, usually at the beginning of October, you can plant out your pot-grown seedlings.

Remember to choose a spot in the appropriate bit of meadow. Place out the pots first, so that they form bold groups of a single species rather than a spotty mixture of different things. Space the plants between 200 and 400mm apart, depending on the eventual scale of the particular species, and when you are sure the layout is right, plant 'em. Ideally you should try and remove a plug of soil just the right size to make room for the pot of roots. If the pot is small enough you might get away with using a bulb-planter to cut out the holes; if not, then a sharp trowel does the job perfectly well. Take the pots off, of course, put the plant roots in the hole, and firm the whole thing with your heel. Don't worry too much about squashing your precious seedlings, they should be quite tough enough to withstand a bit of trampling. Try to avoid leaving any loose soil on the surface of the meadow, or bare earth around the new plants. This is an open invitation for weed seedlings to float in and germinate, and it's the classic way that thistles and dandelions in particular get into meadows. In the countryside it is molehills that often create the problem, and whilst you may well have moles in your lawn, you may as well take the trouble to minimise the risk of weeds by being as tidy as possible when planting.

If the meadow conditions are right, then your wildflowers should multiply year by year. Those which do best will give you a useful clue as to which other species might be worth introducing, and certainly I would suggest that you build up the list gradually by growing a couple of new species each year.

There are one or two meadow wildflowers that are available for planting in a rather more convenient form. These are the meadow bulbs, and you may choose to include quite a few exotic bulbous species in your meadow too, to increase the range of flowers. Wild daffodils, snowflakes, snakehead fritillaries and meadow saffron are all British wildflowers which you can buy as bulbs or corms, though you may have to order from a specialist nursery. It is quite likely that the stock you buy will be of foreign origin, since these plants are all so rare in the wild now, but none of them is likely to leap off and interfere with the surviving fragments of the native population, so unless you live next door to a wild colony, where there actually is a risk that cross-pollination with imported stock could weaken the natives, I think you are quite safe to plant your bulbous wildflowers from whichever nursery source you choose.

If yours is a new garden, then you will need to start your meadow from scratch. In fact, it is not a bad idea to start from bare earth in an established garden if the existing lawn is fertile and vigorous.

The essential requirement for a new wildflower meadow is low fertility. Poverty tends to favour a very wide range of wildflowers, and gives them a bit of an advantage over the more greedy, coarse species. If you're buying a brand-new house, try and get the builder to leave you with a well drained poor sandy subsoil for the meadow if you possibly can. What you normally get is the opposite of this, of course: the worst compaction that twelve months of building site traffic can produce, covered with 150mm of 'topsoil' which has been stockpiled just long enough to build up a really massive bank of dock and thistle seed. If you can get poor soil, all well and good, but if you are landed with highly fertile material then it is worth taking a couple of summers to lower the fertility before you attempt sowing your meadow. Grow a couple of really greedy crops like potatoes or courgettes, and avoid leguminous vegetables like peas and beans because they will actually build up the

Some meadow flowers are quite choosy about the soil they grow in. Cowslips, for instance, do best in a heavy, slightly limy soil. The seed takes several years to germinate too, unless you are lucky enough to be able to sow it absolutely fresh.

nitrogen levels in the soil. When you've harvested your corn on the cob, or dug up your spuds, cart away all the nutrient-rich waste plant material and compost it for use on the permanent vegetable garden. You can speed up the de-fertilizing process by stripping off a layer of the topsoil, too, though the practicality of this remedy rather depends on how big the area is. Certainly it is a good way of preparing an existing over-fertile lawn. Strip the turf, perhaps 75mm or even 100mm thick, and stack it, grass-to-grass until it rots down to form a wonderful crumbly compost for use elsewhere.

Once you have your low-fertility soil, make the drainage as good as you can get it. Of course there are some lovely wildflowers that grow in wet meadows, but unless you can guarantee that your poor drainage is going to be permanent, and isn't just a temporary legacy of the building contractor, it is well worth sorting it out before you begin. Dig a soakaway or two if need be. Just make a deep hole, perhaps a metre or so deep and about the same distance across. Fill this with coarse material – all those half-bricks the builder so thoughtfully left behind for you – and cover the top with a few upside-down turfs and a layer of soil. If you put your soakaways at low points in the garden the 'floodwaters' will run down amongst the bricks and should disappear.

The soil preparation of the seed bed for your well drained, low fertility meadow is perfectly orthodox – just like any normal lawn. The seed will only germinate evenly if the seed bed is fine and crumbly and firm, so you need to rake away until you have broken up all the big lumps, and pulled out all the stones. Shuffle over the whole area to firm the surface, or roll it with a light roller if the area is big enough, and then wait. The best time to sow your meadow seed is late August, with mid-April as a reasonable second choice. You need to allow a gap of at least three weeks between soil preparation and sowing, so that means you should finish your raking at the end of July or in late March. The reason for the three week wait is quite simple. The newly prepared soil will be full of seed already. Within a couple of days, provided it's not too hot and dry, you will see a green sheen develop over your handiwork. The cultivation and sudden exposure to sunlight will have triggered off the germination of thousands and thousands of 'weed' seeds. You may also have bits of root in the soil from such aggressive die-hards as couch grass, creeping thistle and ground elder. Few, if any, of these weed species can survive in an established meadow. They are all very much more efficient than your meadow species at establishing in newly cultivated soil, though, so it is well worth getting rid of as many as possible before you sow. The most efficient way of wiping them out is to wait until the flush of seedlings is about 50mm tall, and then, before any of them have a chance to flower and seed, kill the lot with a non-selective, non-residual systemic weedkiller. Look for something in your garden centre that answers to this description, mix it according to instructions, and apply it from a watering can, taking great care not to let it get on any of the surrounding plants. If, like me, you are suspicious of the so-called 'safe' garden chemicals, and would rather not use them, then you can burn the weed seedlings off with a flame-thrower. These are generally fairly easy to hire these days, and although they look rather terrifying, they will certainly do the trick. The only problem with the non-chemical approach is that it will not deal with the weeds that grow from bits of perennial root. They will just keep coming back for more. There is a third alternative, too, of simply hoeing or raking the seedling crop to uproot and kill it, but that aggravates the perennating root problem more often than not, and it also stirs up another lot of weed seed. In a normal lawn, the regular mowing will quickly get rid of pernicious weeds such as ground elder and couch, but in a meadow, with only a couple of cuts a year, you may be left with a permanent problem. If you have permanent weeds, and your conscience won't let you spray them, even once, then I suggest you adopt a fairly orthodox mowing regime for a couple of seasons, mowing say once every ten days. This will establish a weed-free lawn of fine grasses, and then, when you've mown out the ground elder and couch, you can introduce wildflowers as you would in old, established lawns.

The species you actually choose to sow obviously have a major bearing on the quality of meadow you produce. Essentially, what you are hoping for is a mixture of attractive low-growing, non-aggressive grasses, and a selection of wildflowers that suit your chosen mowing regime. There are any number of pre-selected seed mixes available, but really there is only one golden rule. Whatever else you do, never sow a mixture which contains ryegrass. This is the tough, wiry grass used to produce hardwearing sports pitches and play lawns. It must be kept out of your meadow. The grasses you do want all have relatively small seeds, and since you want to leave plenty of gaps for the wildflowers to germinate, the second important rule is to sow very small quantities. You can produce a very good-looking meadow simply by selecting a 'no-ryegrass' mixture straight off the shelf at your local garden centre, and sowing it at about one fifth the recommended rate. That is actually quite difficult, since you are talking about little more than a pinch or two to the square metre. You can make sowing evenly at these very low rates easier by mixing the seed very thoroughly indeed with sawdust or silver sand. This has the double advantage of giving the different sized seeds an extra mix, to counter any separating out that might have taken place in the packet, and also giving you a much clearer picture of where you have actually sown. Your grass mix should contain at least three or four non-rye species. Red fescue (*Festuca rubra*), common bent (*Agrostis tenuis*) and smooth meadow grass (*Poa pratense*) are all fairly standard, and then you might like to add one or two specifically hay-meadow species such as meadow foxtail (*Alopecuris pratensis*), timothy (*Phleum pratense*) and Yorkshire fog (*Holcus lanatus*). To give your meadow that very special 'new-mown hay' smell you need to include a little sweet vernal grass (*Anthoxanthemum odoratum*) too. If you are sowing in the late summer, as I suggested, then you can use a very simple, standard fine grasses mix and spice it up a bit by visiting the nearest attractive stretch of unmown roadside verge and collecting a handful or two of the seed of those grasses you like the look of. The total weight of fine grass seed you need to sow is no more than 2gms per square metre, and that is why it is so helpful to bulk it up with a carrier. In fact, to get a really even coverage I find it is worth dividing the quantity of seed into two halves, and sowing one half in one direction, and then broadcasting the other portion at right angles to it. After the grass seed has been sown, you can then oversow with the seed of various wildflowers. With these I think it is better to deal with individual species, and sow them either in drifts on their own, or mixed in very simple combinations of two or three species. This means that you can sow cheap, predictably successful species such as moonpenny or ox-eye daisy (*Chrysanthemum leucanthemum*) and yellow rattle (*Rhianthus minor*) over the whole area, and restrict the more precious seed to pockets where they will be particularly valuable, or particularly well-suited to some peculiarity of the site, such as a wet patch or a shaded area. I definitely favour a fairly simple range of wildflowers for starters, with more species added as pot-grown seedlings when the meadow has settled down. For the spring meadow I would start with cowslip (*Primula veris*), speedwell (*Veronica chamaedrys*), cat's ear (*Hypochoeris radiata*), selfheal (*Prunella vulgaris*), hoary plantain (*Plantago media*), common sorrel (*Rumex acetosa*), salad burnet (*Poterium sanguisorba*) and a generous proportion of ox-eye daisy. For the late summer meadow I would still include ox-eye daisy, because it looks so marvellous in early summer, and should survive. Other basic species include meadow buttercup (*Ranunculus acris*), lady's bedstraw (*Galium verum*), wild carrot (*Daucus carota*), common knapweed (*Centaurea nigra*), field scabious (*Knautia arvensis*) and meadow cranesbill (*Geranium pratense*).

When all the seed has been sown, run gently over the surface of the seed bed with the back of a rake, to cover the seed lightly. Then refirm the whole thing either by treading or by light rolling. Finally, stretch some lengths of cotton across from side to side, with twists of aluminium foil or newspaper tied in to scare away the sparrows. Ideal conditions for germination are dull, drizzly weather, so you might like to make certain of that by booking your holidays for the week following sowing. If the weather is very dry, then it is worth watering, but do be careful to avoid washing the surface and disturbing the seed. If you get it right, the soil should be really thoroughly soaked by a continuous fine spray. If you get

My meadow, grown from seed, flowered beautifully in its second summer, though most of the colour came from just two or three species.

it wrong, then seed will germinate in pretty, wave-shaped narrow bands.

All being well, an August sowing will give you a good covering of grass before the winter, though most of the wildflowers will stay dormant until the spring. If the growth gets any taller than 75mm, then it is advisable to go over it with a mower, and chop off the tops. Don't cut any lower than 50mm, and do, please, make sure you use a sharp mower or shears, as the seedlings are still very weak. The roots will not be very well established and a blunt lawnmower can pull the plants out of the soil. Go over the area with a light roller, or firm feet, immediately after cutting, to push back any loosened plants. In the first year after sowing you should expect very little in the way of flowers. The seed will germinate, but the plants will mainly be producing root and leaf. For this reason there is nothing to be lost by mowing through the summer, and in fact, this is quite a good idea in the first year. Set the blade as high as it will go, and keep taking the clippings off. This will encourage the grasses to spread, and will concentrate all the plant's energy into root establishment. In the second spring after sowing you can adopt your permanent mowing cycle, and you should be rewarded with a really colourful display of flowers. In the first year of my sown meadow one or two ox-eye daisies managed to bloom, but in the second summer the wildflowers completely dominated the meadow for week after week.

You may be wondering what to cut your meadow with. Certainly it is not easy fighting your way through two-foot tall grass with a little manual cylinder mower. The best tool of all is probably a scythe, and if you are feeling energetic it will give you a tremendous sense of satisfaction to see the swathes of hay falling away beneath your blades. Scything is marvellous for the waistline, too – which probably tells you that I use a mowing machine myself. In fact, the best machine of all is a motor-scythe with what is called a reciprocating blade. This works like a vicious-looking row of scissors, and actually cuts through the stems. Alternatively you can use a strimmer. That is one of those modern machines that has a length of nylon thread at the business end, which whizzes round at a terrifying rate and slices through everything but the patio windows in the TV adverts. The fourth option is a rotary mower, but you need one with wheels so that you can set the blades high, and it really has to be pretty hefty to cope. Remember you are only going to have the problem once or possibly twice a year. What I would do is stick to your existing mower for cutting the lawn, and if it isn't powerful enough for the meadow, and you aren't powerful enough for the scythe, then I suggest you hire an appropriate machine for the two days each year.

When you have cut the hay, leave it on the surface for a day or two before taking it off – this allows it to dry, the wildflowers can shed their ripe seed, and any caterpillars and other meadow mini-beasts that have

survived the mowing can migrate down into the stubble and out of harm's way. You must remove the hay eventually, though. Put it on the compost heap, or use it as bedding for the local hamster population.

There is one final, and very obvious thing to say about meadow management. Having established your low fertility, high species diversity grassland community, don't spray it with chemicals. No matter what the experts tell you about autumn lawn dressings and the horror of the leatherjackets, remember that your meadow is there to provide a habitat for wildlife. If you are ever in the slightest doubt, just take five minutes to watch the swallows swooping backwards and forwards over the grass and flowers and look down into the tangle of stems at the mass of different creatures living there, or sit quietly in the magic half-hour just after nightfall and listen to the squeaks and scuffles in your new habitat. That's the way you will know your meadow is successful. The fact that it looks more and more beautiful each summer is just a very welcome bonus.

Chapter 7

Garden ponds and other 'wetlands'

A WILDLIFE garden without a pond is like a theatre without a stage. The woodland-edge habitat and the mini-meadow create the 'countryside' atmosphere, certainly, and the wildlife they support is fascinating, but the real thrills, the real dramas of the rich habitat garden take place in and around the pond. I sit for hours every summer, captivated by the aerobatics of the dragonflies that hunt, mate and lay their eggs there. In the depths of winter, when snow covers the whole neighbourhood, I am entertained day after day by the squabbling, splashing crowds of starlings and other birds which bathe in the icy shallows. Winter bathing is essential, apparently, to give the plumage maximum fluffability on killingly cold nights. Mini-wetlands in towns have proved more than anything else, that urban nature conservation really can provide some positive compensation for habitat destruction in the countryside. The common frog in particular would be virtually extinct by now were it not for the gnome-fringed ponds of suburbia, and the same will soon be true of diving beetles, damselflies, pondskaters and many more of the fascinating creatures that rely for their survival on small stretches of unpolluted, shallow water. The ponds of the countryside have mostly been filled in now. The ditches have been piped to make way for bigger, combinable fields, and those wetlands that do survive are suffering terribly from fertiliser run-off and chemical over-spray. A garden pond provides you with a guaranteed means of helping wildlife survive, and the life it brings to your doorstep will enrich every aspect of the enjoyment your garden gives you.

British wetland habitats are especially important for international conservation. Bird migration is particularly dependent on our estuaries, lakes and marshes, with visiting wildfowl travelling here in vast numbers each autumn to escape the frozen winters of northern Russia, Greenland and Scandinavia. In the summer our wet woodlands provide nesting

OVERLEAF: A pond really does make the perfect centrepiece to the wildlife garden.

habitat for willow warblers from Africa, the soft mud around our lakes and ponds is used for nest-building by migrant housemartins, eroded river cliffs are the natural nesting sites for sand martins, and of course the constant supply of newly-hatched mayflies, midges and other aquatic insects provide the thousands of swallows and swifts that visit us with a large proportion of their high-protein diet. One of the most spectacular urban wildlife sights I know is the latterday Battle of Britain that takes place every day throughout the summer, where the sewers meet the Thames at Kingston. Tens of thousands of swifts, swallows and martins swoop and dive with breathtaking agility as they snap up the clouds of insects amongst the buses and lorries on the A307.

Massive post-war building programmes have created some new wetlands, to compensate for the loss of lakes and ponds elsewhere. All that tarmac and concrete takes a great deal of gravel, and all those extra people drink a lot of water. Along many flood plains you will find wet gravel pits, and there have been a good many new reservoirs built this century, too. With care the new wetlands can become immensely rich wildlife sanctuaries, and in fact the gravel pits in particular have provided us with most of our new wetland habitat creation techniques. There are very sophisticated research projects studying little else at Great Linford in Milton Keynes, and in Sevenoaks, Kent.

The open, deep water of reservoirs and glacial lakes is of relatively little wildlife value, though it does provide a safe roost for the large flocks of urban 'seagulls'. In fact, in London, by failing to consider seagull ecology the planners have created quite a traffic hazard, as thousands of big, engine-clogging birds commute twice daily across airport flight paths from the reservoir roosts to their feeding grounds on the rubbish tips.

It is really the shallow waters that are the great wildlife resource. Most of the wild plants and animals live in the relative warmth amongst the reeds and rushes of the reservoir margin, and even the deepwater fish tend to move into the safety of the shallows to breed. Wetlands don't stop at the water's edge either. Flood meadows, marshes, wet pasture and waterlogged willow and alder woodland are all vitally important to their own particular dependent community of wild plants and animals. Sadly, these habitats have probably suffered even more than the ponds and ditches in recent years. Land drainage is now relatively easy with the powerful machinery we have available. Well-drained land is agricultur-ally more productive than marshy ground. Farmers can grow potatoes and wheat where previously they could perhaps only graze cattle for part of the year. The Ministry of Agriculture and the Drainage Authorities have poured hundreds of millions of pounds into agricultural land drainage – lowering watertables, straightening rivers and destroying wetland habitat. The result of all this devastating public spending is that where we once had wildlife lakes, we now have milk lakes.

Even without all the deliberate destruction, wetlands are particularly vulnerable. Ponds and lakes are all gradually silting up as the rainwater washes particles of soil from high ground down to the lowlands. Leaf litter accumulates, and sooner or later the wetland will turn into dryland. I spent my childhood playing in an old industrial river valley on the edge of Sheffield. In its heyday, at the end of the nineteenth century, that stream had been harnessed for water power by building a whole chain of millponds, but by the time I came on the scene half a century later, almost every one had silted up completely and was supporting a dense tangle of tall willow and alder trees. Of course the old mill managers would never have let that happen. They would have employed men to keep the races clear, dredge out the silt and cut back the overhanging trees, but when steam and then electric power overtook the waterwheel, the wetlands were abandoned, and nature reclaimed the land.

Now, at last, the single-mindedness of agricultural land drainage seems to be tempered by a growing public demand for commonsense. Over the last couple of years we have seen farmers burning effigies of Nature Conservancy Council officers on the Somerset levels, because they dared to decide that the value of the wet meadows as an over-wintering ground for 20,000 migratory ducks, geese, swans and waders was of more importance to the nation than the highly profitable additions to the butter, wheat and potato mountains which the farmers could have made following publicly-funded land drainage. This followed close on the heels of an encouraging incident in the Ribble Valley, where the threat of large-scale land drainage was countered when the Royal Society for the Protection of Birds was given a large government grant to help buy the land. The row which developed over one landowner's wish to drain the last surviving stretch of once extensive Norfolk marshland at Halvergate helped bring the whole issue of habitat destruction for personal gain firmly into the limelight, and there seems a chance that we might now manage to cling on to those few wet bits of countryside that still survive.

All of this may seem rather remote from the issue of garden ponds, gnomes with fishing rods, and jam jars full of frogspawn, but it seems to me that the two ends of the wetland story are undeniably linked. The more people there are in towns who have had the first hand thrill of seeing an ugly brown creature crawl laboriously up the stem of a flag iris and heave itself clumsily into a new life as a dazzling blue damsel fly, or have gasped as the early morning sun picked out the beautiful, tattered pink flowers of the ragged robin, the more chance we have of winning the battle for conservation of our rare, precious and fast disappearing wetlands in the countryside.

Creating a garden wetland is probably easier now than it has ever been. The great revolution in garden ponds has come with the development of flexible waterproof sheet liners, and with a bit of manipulation these can be used to create bogs and marshes as well as pools. Choose a part of your garden which is reasonably sheltered and, preferably, easily visible from inside the house. If you have your wetland fairly close to the building, then you may be able to tap into the rainwater guttering, and there is no doubt that the best artificial wetlands are those kept wet by rainwater. Generally speaking, it is best to choose a position which is light and sunny. There *are* wild creatures that inhabit the gloomy, leaf-filled pools of deepest woodland, but you will certainly have more colourful action if you go for a 'light' pond. If your garden slopes, try to choose a spot for the wetland at the lower end. It isn't absolutely crucial, but artificial ponds and marshes always look more convincing if they lie in a natural hollow or at the bottom of a slope. Avoid wet hollows for artificial ponds: though that may seem like the most perfect place, you will curse when you have to dig underwater. You will have nowhere to drain to, either, and that could well give you a flood problem in wet weather. If you have a naturally wet hollow, plant that with marsh plants and put the pond slightly higher up the slope; then it can overflow into the natural wetland.

Avoid overhanging trees if you can. For one thing, the autumn leaves really are a nuisance. You will inevitably get some in your pond, even in a quite treeless garden, but overhanging branches guarantee difficulties ahead. The other reason for avoiding trees is that your excavations will damage the roots. It can be rather embarrassing if you site your pond to reflect the 'wonderful sculptural form of the mature beech tree', and then the mature beech tree promptly keels over and dies.

The ideal setting from the wildlife point of view would be a south-west facing corner of the garden, where part of the shoreline can be tucked into the dense undergrowth of the woodland edge, and the remainder can sit naturally in the meadow grassland. Paved or mown access to one or two parts of the pond edge will give you the chance to watch the wildlife at close quarters, and the adjacent shrubbery will provide a sheltered, safe approach for the more timid of your garden creatures.

When you've chosen the ideal spot for your mini-wetland, I'm afraid you have no alternative but to face up to the next rather strenuous stage. You will have to dig a big hole. Do make absolutely sure you are happy with the siting before you start. Digging is hard work, but filling in again is even harder.

I marked out the shape of my pond with some canes first, and left them for a week or two. This helped me visualise the new pond and marsh, and, in fact, I did alter the shape and the position quite a lot before I finally dug the hole.

I really can't enthuse strongly enough about how marvellous a garden

OPPOSITE: This little bubbling fountain is absolutely safe for children and still provides wildlife garden visitors with a supply of water for drinking and bathing. It is made simply by placing a submersible electric pump in an artificially lined puddle, and covering the lot with big pebbles.

The easiest and most successful way to create artificial wetlands is to use a flexible waterproof liner. Protect your butyl sheeting or polythene both above and below, and cover the whole thing with at least 100mm of sandy subsoil. Make sure there are plenty of shallow marginal areas and some waterlogged marshy ground. Some part of the pond should also be at least 600mm deep. Bats, damselflies and dragonflies will hunt for small insects over the surface of the pond. All kinds of creatures will spend part of their lifecycle in the water – damselfly larvae, waterboatmen, frogs and tadpoles, dragonflies and their larvae, sticklebacks, pondskaters and pondsnails.

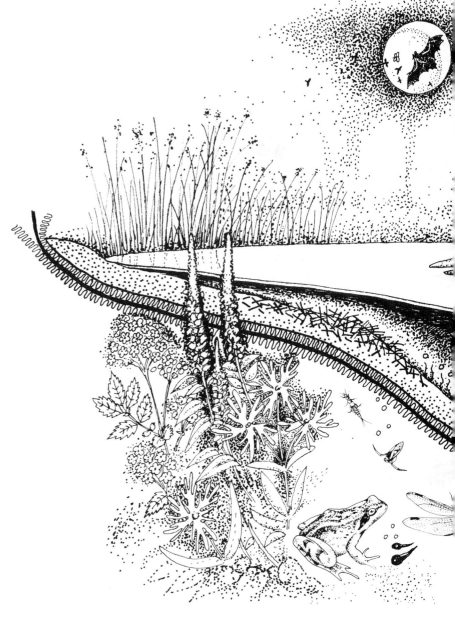

pond is. When you are deciding how large yours should be, go for the biggest you can afford. Mind you, having said that, I had a tiny pond in my very first garden which I made by sinking a 600mm square water tank into the ground, and even that was full of life in no time. To get the best habitat possible, you should allow for at least one area where the pond is very shallow. If you cover the liner to bring the soil back up to top water-level, then you will be able to grow marsh plants in the waterlogged conditions. The other absolutely critical characteristics of a first class wildlife pond are very shallow edges, and a depth of at least 600mm somewhere in the centre. The ideal shape of hole you should dig is a very

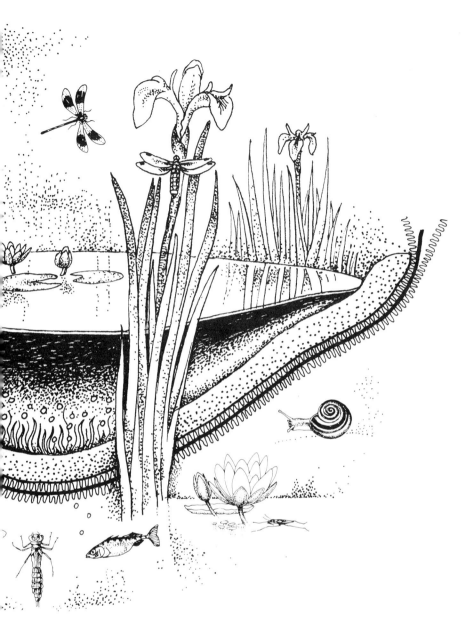

gently sided saucer, and if you are going to get down to the depth I suggest, then you will need a fairly big area. The minimum depth is necessary to allow pond life to survive below a sheet of the very thickest ice in the coldest of winters, and the shallow edges are crucial as a habitat for many of the wetland water plants, and also as a safe access route for the wildlife that climbs in and out of the pond. It also makes the whole thing much safer when uninitiated infants decide to try and walk on the water.

If you are lucky enough to have a stream in your garden, then you can create a pond and marsh relatively simply by building a dam. Before you

OVERLEAF: It is tiny ponds like this which have saved the rural frog population from near extinction.

do, though, you really should discuss this with the Local Council or the Drainage Authority. You may need to take professional advice on the structure, too, if you are attempting anything more ambitious than a railway sleeper or a pile of four or five sandbags. Even a small pool contains a surprising volume of water, and if your inadequate dam bursts, you will be liable for any damage the flood water causes downstream.

Most of us have gardens without streams. In this case you have a choice of four different methods for water-proofing your wetland. Traditionally, you would have used clay. Puddled clay is the sticky material that keeps the water in most of our canals, and it works very well, provided it isn't allowed to dry out and crack. You may be fortunate in having a local source of supply, in which case it's worth a try, but if you have to start paying for transport, then I strongly suggest you choose a cheaper, more reliable alternative. Ideally, the clay should be laid in blocks a bit like brick paving. Pack the blocks tightly together, water them and then 'puddle' for all you are worth. You need to trample the wet sticky clay really thoroughly until it smears together and forms a watertight lining. The old navigators apparently used to drive herds of cows and flocks of sheep along the bed of their new clay-lined canals to puddle them in. You might prefer to invite all the kids in the neighbourhood round, and tell them on no account to set foot in the new pond – that should do the trick. You can actually buy your clay lining in a bagged, powdered form these days. The material is known as Bentonite, and it is used by engineers for waterproofing very large reservoirs, so it should be more than adequate for your garden pond. The difficulty seems to be in getting a complete and even covering, and the manufacturers have recently come up with the idea of impregnating a fabric with the clay. You spread this across the bottom of your pond-excavation, with the joints firmly overlapped, and when you add water the clay becomes sticky and forms an impervious, waterproof layer.

For years, most people built their garden ponds of concrete. If you have inherited one, the odds are it now leaks, and that is the main problem. Concrete is very strong under pressure, but it cracks under tension very easily, and you only need a bit of uneven settlement, or an exceptional frost, to fracture the concrete. The other thing that puts me off concrete pool construction is the speed at which you have to work. A couple of cubic metres of ready-mix doesn't sound much when you order it over the phone, but when the mixer lorry plugs its rear end into your front garden, and the driver pulls the handle, the avalanche that follows seems to go on forever. You are then faced with a marathon task, equivalent to anything the sorcerer's apprentice had to cope with, racing up and down with wheelbarrows, stopping every now and again to ponder why the pile in the drive seems to get bigger rather than smaller, and then to pray that it might rain, and slow down the alarming pace at which the concrete seems to be setting.

You need at least a 100mm layer of concrete over the whole of the inside of your pond, and you cannot really knock off half-way through and start again the next day – at least not without involving yourself in some pretty sophisticated engineering work. You can reduce the risk of cracking by making sure the ground below the concrete is as rock-solid as you can get it, and then by incorporating some reinforcing mesh in the concrete as you lay it. You cannot use metal rods and mesh generally, because the contours of your pool are likely to be curved, so you need to use a flexible material. Heavy gauge galvanised chicken netting is quite good. You've probably used it for the front of rabbit hutches, or to protect your rows of peas in the past and it is quite cheap if you buy a whole roll from the hardware shop. As an alternative you can use a heavy grade of nylon netting – the sort you might use for a tennis net.

Pay particular attention to the shape of the concrete at the lip of your pond. It needs to be level all the way round, of course, otherwise the water will run out at the lowest point and leave you with embarrassingly ugly mini-cliffs at all the high spots. It also needs to slope outwards. This isn't just a detail which makes life easier for bathing hedgehogs to clamber in and out, it has a structural function, too. Concrete is very weak under tension, remember. When the water freezes you will obviously get a slab of ice on the surface, and as it freezes it will expand. If the edges at the top are vertical, the swollen ice will push the walls apart, and crack the concrete. If you have gentle slopes, then the ice is much more likely simply to slide up as it expands and leave the concrete undamaged.

There is one particular precaution you have to take with concrete. You can get toxic chemicals in the water when the new pond is first filled. These evaporate or precipitate out after a few weeks, but it is worth changing the water a month or so after you first fill it, and you must allow at least that length of time before you begin to introduce any pond life.

The third option is a pre-formed rigid fibreglass or plastic pond. You will find these stacked against the wall at your local garden centre or aquatic specialists, and they come in all shapes and sizes. As a relatively foolproof method of keeping the water in they are excellent. You still have to dig the hole, of course, but you don't have to worry so much about settlement, and the job is certainly a lot quicker and less strenuous than either concrete or clay. Preformed ponds have two disadvantages as wildlife habitat, apart that is from the fact that, despite the apparently infinite choice, you never seem to be able to find the shape you need. The first problem is the edge profile. All these ponds seem to have vertical sides which stand up at least 100mm and often higher. This really is quite an obstacle for many of the smaller amphibians and for any mammals

Some of our loveliest wildflowers grow best at the water's-edge. Yellow flag-iris (*Iris pseudacorus* above) prefers wet soil, whilst the Burr reed (*Sparganium spp,* opposite) is a marginal plant that will happily grow in 200mm of water.

that tumble in, though you can overcome the problem to some extent by piling rocks on the ledge inside the pond, and providing a route out that way. The other difficulty is caused by the steep slope and the shiny finish. These combine to make it almost impossible to cover the bottom with soil or gravel, and that makes the pond pretty hostile to wildlife. You are left with no alternative but to grow your water plants in pots or baskets standing on the bottom, and whilst this makes them easier to keep under control, it never produces the tangle of underwater vegetation that creates such vital shelter for the smaller pond creatures.

I think by far the best waterproofing method is the flexible sheet liner. There are now several different grades available. 1000 gauge black polythene is the cheapest option that works. There are plastic sheets which have a tough terylene mesh incorporated into them for extra protection against ripping, and at the Rolls Royce end of the market there is a very tough rubberised fabric liner known as butyl sheeting. Butyl is the toughest by far, and can be expected to last for forty or fifty years at least. The other two materials can work very well too, but you must adopt a technique of using them which protects them adequately from sunlight. The ultra-violet rays can make exposed polythene brittle enough to crack and leak within a summer, even through two or three feet of murky pond water.

I recommend the same technique for all the different sheetliners, and so far it has proved pretty successful. You need to excavate your wetland at least 150mm deeper all over than the eventual depth you want your pond water to be. If you want a shallow margin with 100mm of water in it, dig down 250mm. If the deepest point in the centre is to be 600mm deep, dig down 750mm and so on. Remember to shape the excavation so that it has gently sloping contours only. Don't leave any sharp changes of direction that would be difficult for the liner to follow. Excavate the ground 150mm deep for half a metre or so all around the edge of the pool, too. You will need the overlap to anchor the liner, and do check and double check that the edge is the same level all the way round.

Once the shape is right, go over the whole surface, carefully removing any sharp stones, bits of broken glass or china or anything else which might work its way up and puncture the liner from beneath. The next task is to spread a cushioning layer of some material or another over the whole of the excavated surface, as an extra precaution against puncturing. 50mm of the 150mm extra digging is there to allow you to spread a layer of sand in the hole. That is one of the cheapest materials you can use. There are various alternatives. Old carpets are very good. Lots of tough old polythene sacks, sheets of dampened cardboard or thick pads of folded newspaper, will all help. The best material of all is a polypropylene matting specially made for the job. It is very tough – virtually impenetrable – but it does cost rather a lot.

Run your protective layer up and over the lip of the hole. The edges are obviously the most likely parts to get punctured, because there is the added pressure of careless feet to contend with. Once you are satisfied that the bed of the wetland is puncture-proof, spread your sheet liner out on the lawn, carry it across and stretch it over the hole. Make sure you've allowed plenty of overlap, and then weight down the edges with smooth-bottomed heavy objects. Bricks are ideal.

Now here my recommendations differ from those of most people. All the books say you should put the hose pipe into the middle of the sheet, turn on the tap, and let the weight of the water stretch the liner down to hug the walls of the pond. That does work very well, but it leaves you with the liner shining up at you through the water, and it is very difficult to cover it effectively with a sunshine-filtering, protective layer of anything. I prefer to ease the liner into the hole gradually, under its own weight. I then spread a further protective layer of matting, folded newspaper or the equivalent on top of my liner, making sure that if I need to step into the hole I always tread on a protected bit, and as the liner is covered over, I complete the protection by shovelling in an over layer of subsoil or gravel. The waterproof liner is securely anchored under 150mm of soil all around the edge, and I am then left with an empty waterproof hole, lined with an impervious sheet sandwiched between soft protective layers of padding and soil.

The last stage in the operation is obviously the filling. With soil at the bottom, you don't want simply to splash the hose pipe in – you will end up with a mud bath. What I do is rest the hosepipe on top of a square of polythene or a piece of the protective matting, and let the water trickle in over that. It is a trick I learned from watching Arab nurserymen in the Middle East watering their tree-seedlings with a three inch hose, and it should be possible for you to fill the pond completely without stirring up the soil in the bottom.

The best time to plant up your wetland is April or early May, though with pot-grown garden centre plants you can do it at any time. There is little point bothering in winter, though. Almost all the plants die down to nothing in the autumn, and the thought of having to break through the ice to put in the plants isn't my idea of fun. You have to get into the water to plant properly, and this can be pretty chilly. If you have a layer of soil in your pond, plant straight into it. This may mean your waterplants run a bit wild, but they are easy enough to control if they get out of hand, and you are aiming to establish a healthy habitat as rapidly as possible. If you have chosen a concrete or pre-formed pond, then plant into those perforated plastic containers.

The plants you need to introduce fall into several categories, and again you will produce the richest habitat if you stick to native species. That really is no hardship with wetlands. Our indigenous marshland and pond plants are very beautiful indeed. The first and most essential category of plants is the submerged large green algae. These are generally sold in bundles, often tied with a strip of lead to weight them down and you will find them under the label 'oxygenators'. These are the plants that spread across the bottom of the pool and provide a hiding place and food source for most of the smallest pond creatures. Although you can just lob them into the water and trust in the lead to carry them down to the bottom, I prefer to anchor them more firmly. Try and stick some of the cut ends into the soil, and then make sure they stay put with a half brick. These filamentous green plants are very buoyant, and if you don't take this precaution you are likely to find them all floating on the surface again half an hour later. It is infinitely preferable to get your submerged oxygenators from some other established pond, rather than in bundles from a nursery if you can. Most pond-owners will be happy to rake you out a bucketful, particularly later in the spring or summer, when it is growing well, and you have the possibility of gaining a bonus in the form of pond snail eggs or even more exciting mini-beasts. Beware, though. Some passengers are not quite so welcome. Check that the donor-pond doesn't have any blanket weed in it. You will probably get it sooner or later anyway, but there is no point in actively encouraging its introduction. Watch out for the more vicious predators, too. Diving beetle larvae hide in pondweed, and again you don't really want to introduce such aggressive residents at this early stage. One exotic aquatic that you should definitely try to avoid is Canadian pondweed (*Elodaea canadensis*). This is much more vigorous than native oxygenators such as millfoil and water starwort, and will take over the pond in no time. It isn't the end of the world if you do introduce it. You just have to spend a lot more time pulling out piles of it with a wire rake.

There are one or two rather nice water plants which grow with their roots in the bottom, and their leaves floating on the surface half a metre or more above. For large pools you can't beat the native water lilies, yellow and white, and for smaller pools I think there are few more valuable and attractive plants than amphibious bistort, with its pretty pink flowers, and the common pond weed. Both have very similar oval, olive green leaves, and look lovely growing together. The fringed water-lily is a useful plant for a small pond, too. Its leaves are more or less circular and only 50mm or so across, and it has beautiful, simple yellow flowers emerging one after another throughout the summer.

When you reach the shallows there is a terrific choice of the plants we call 'emergents'. They all seem to have a preference for a particular depth of water, but in a garden pond they will tend to find their own level pretty quickly. At the deep end, bog bean (*Menyanthes trifoliata*) is perhaps the plant whose flower I love the most. It makes up for its rather slapstick

> ## NATIVE WILDFLOWERS FOR THE POND
>
> **Marginal Plants**
> **The marsh plants will all grow happily around the edge of the pond. The following will cope with water as much as 150mm deep.**
>
> **Yellow iris** (*Iris pseudacorus*) Very beautiful wildflower with wonderful bright green sword-like leaves, and yellow flowers which bloom through June, and are followed by pods of brown seeds. Can be very invasive, but there are always people around eager to adopt a clump or two.
>
> **Water mint** (*Mentha aquatica*) Aromatic leaves, and lovely pink flowers which attract butterflies in August and September.
>
> **Water plantain** (*Alisma plantago-aquatica*) Pretty little pale lilac flowers on wiry tiered stems. Seeds and colonises the shallows rapidly.
>
> **Brooklime** (*Veronica beccabunga*) Bright blue flowers on fleshy-leaved prostrate stems.
>
> **Water forget-me-not** (*Myosotis scorpioides*) Pale blue and beautiful.
>
> **Lesser spearwort** (*Ranunculus flammula*) A delicate little yellow 'buttercup' which creeps around in the shallows. Looks particularly beautiful when the electric blue damselflies settle on them.

Do try to include a waterlogged marshy area. This purple loosestrife (*Lythrum salicaria*) gives a wonderful display of magenta flowers on 2 metre spikes in August, and obviously the butterflies like it too.

name by producing a spike of the most exquisite, feathery white flowers in June. Its three-lobed blue-green leaves look rather like those of broad bean and it seems to grow happily in water as deep as 600mm. There are a couple of other emergents that will grow up through quite deep water, but you should avoid them in a garden pond. One is the plant most people call bullrush. Technically it should be called greater reedmace or *Typha latifolia*. The other is *Phragmites communis*, the common reed, and that is even more of a nuisance. Once established it just spreads like mad, and overwhelms everything else. If you can't live without bull-rushes, then try the more slender, elegant and less aggressive lesser reedmace, *Typha angustifolia*.

Around the very shallow margins of the pond you can grow several plants which are both beautiful and valuable for wildlife. Yellow flag iris (*Iris pseudacorus*) is one which I am particularly fond of, though it does need controlling firmly. Flowering rush (*Butomus umbellatus*) is much less invasive, and it really must be one of our most beautiful wildflowers. When its cluster of coral-pink flowers is blooming, visitors to the garden will never believe that it is a native – a water weed. Water plantain, water mint (*Mentha aquatica*) and the burr reeds (*Sparganium* spp) all grow happily with their 'feet' in a few centimetres of water, and all of them are fast disappearing in the wild. One shallow water emergent which needs treating with caution is the greater spearwort (*Ranunculus lingua*). This is one of the most spectacular of all the buttercup family, growing a metre tall and carrying a pure yellow flower at the top of a handsome stem. It has become very rare in the wild, but in garden ponds it seems to go berserk, sending out long horizontal underwater shoots and springing up all over the place. I put three small pieces in the shallows the first spring, and by the following summer there was a spearwort forest decorating half the pond. The flower is very beautiful, though, particularly when it is chosen as the perch for a turquoise-blue darter dragonfly, and it is really very easy to weed out any unwanted stems every now and again.

The marshy, waterlogged ground around the edges of ponds is an important habitat for another range of equally attractive wildflowers, and I am delighted with the colour my artificial marshland brings to the summer garden. In the band of meadow which is under-laid with pondliner, and therefore kept permanently moist, I can grow the more delicate marsh-grassland flowers, and the shallow arm of the pond which I filled in with soil again up to water level provides an ideal habitat for the taller marsh plants proper.

Along the damp grass margin I now have ribbons of brilliant blue and yellow all summer long. The blue is a mixture of water veronica or brooklime (*Veronica becca-bunga*) and water forget-me-not (*Myosotis*

Toads bred in our pond in the second spring. Here the male clings on to the much larger female, and fertilises the long string of toadspawn which then sinks to the bottom. Garden ponds really have made a difference to the survival of our amphibians.

NATIVE WILDFLOWERS FOR THE MARSH

Purple loosestrife (*Lythrum salicaria*) A dramatic plant producing tall, slender spikes of mauve flowers up to 2 metres tall. Very popular with bees and large white butterflies.

Meadowsweet (*Filipendula ulmaria*) Lovely summery perfume from clouds of fluffy cream flower-heads. Grows about 1½ metres tall and attracts lots of bees.

Salad burnet (*Sanguisorba minor*) An unusual wildflower with edible leaves that taste of walnuts. Purple flowers and fresh green cut-leaves.

Ragged robin (*Lychnis flos-cuculi*) One of the most beautiful of our wildflowers – growing best in wet meadows. A lovely 'tattered' pink flower which blooms all summer long.

Meadow buttercup (*Ranunculus acris*) Much more handsome than the creeping buttercup. Tall, branched flower stems a metre tall, and delicate palmate leaves.

Hemp agrimony (*Eupatorium cannabinum*) One of the very best butterfly plants. Grows 1–2 metres tall, produces flat heads of pink flowers, which develop into fluffy seedheads.

Codlins and Cream or Hairy willowherb (*Epilobium hirsutum*) A lovely loose habit, and masses of deep pink flowers with a cream centre. Popular with bees, but producing clouds of fluffy seeds and colonising rapidly.

Marsh marigold (*Caltha palustris*) Big yellow buttercup flowers on good solid foliage about 300mm tall. Avoid the double-flowered form, which is sterile and doesn't set seed.

Marsh woundwort (*Stachys palustris*) Similar flower to hedge woundwort – deep purple brown and good for bees.

Bugle (*Ajuga reptans*) A prostrate, creeping evergreen plant which is shade-tolerant and produces 150mm tall spikes of blue flowers. Very good for bees and butterflies.

Creeping jenny (*Lysimachia nummularia*) Pale green leaves on long creeping stems, punctuated with bright yellow little flowers.

scorpioides) and the yellow is a close relative of the invasive giant buttercup, this one growing only 150mm or so tall and going by the name of lesser spearwort (*Ranunculus flammula*). Creeping along at damp ground level there is also the bugle flower (*Ajuga reptans*) with its purple spikes so popular with insects, and the delicate little yellow creeping jenny (*Lysimachia nummularia*). In a wildlife garden in Switzerland I saw clumps of that most beautiful of wildflowers, grass of Parnassus (*Parnassia palustris*), growing on the grassy edge of an artificial pond, so I will be growing that from seed this year, to add to the habitat.

In the deeper, soggier soil of the marsh proper there is room to grow the vigorous, wetland wildflowers that you see now mainly in overgrown ditches in the more remote parts of Britain. Most of them flower in August, though there is a bit of colour earlier on. One of the prettiest of plants is ragged robin (*Lychnis flos-cuculi*) with its bunches of delicate pink flowers. That flowers in June and deserves a place in every garden. It is now one of our officially 'threatened' wildflowers. By midsummer my marsh is over a metre and half tall, and a riot of frothy pinks and whites. Meadow sweet (*Filipendula ulmaria*) has a lovely summery perfume, and pretty little cream flowers, a bit like elder. Purple loosestrife (*Lythrum salicaria*) sends up spectacular spikes of magenta blossoms which look particularly dramatic when they attract the odd white butterfly. Hemp agrimony (*Eupatorium cannabinum*) is another marvellous butterfly plant, particularly popular with bees as well, and hairy willowherb, which I prefer to call by its much more romantic alternative name of codlins and cream (*Epilobium hirsutum*), completes the picture. If you have room for a waterside shrub then you could do worse than plant bog myrtle. It prefers slightly acid, peaty soil, but the aroma from its leaves is delicious.

One of the most fascinating things about creating a new pond is the way in which aquatic animal life manages to colonise it unaided. You will be amazed by the variety of pond insects that arrive from nowhere, almost as soon as the water goes into the pond. Pond skaters and whirlygig beetles are normally the first to arrive, but in no time at all you can expect to have diving beetles, water boatmen and masses of wriggly little larvae, too. Dragonflies are very mobile, and may well have been visiting your garden in search of insect prey for years, but damselflies and one or two of the other desirable water creatures don't travel so much, and you may need to introduce them. Resist this temptation for a year at least, though, and enjoy the pleasure of seeing what turns up on its own.

As suggested earlier, the introduced water plants will provide the vehicle for quite a lot of the smaller creatures, and certainly a good many eggs will arrive that way. The round-ended oblong blocks of jelly are

---

NATIVE WILDFLOWERS FOR THE POND

Emergent plants

These wildflowers will grow in deeper water and send their leaves and flower stems up above the water surface.

Bog bean (*Menyanthes trifoliata*) The most delicate of white flowers, standing above strong, blue-green leaves that look like broad beans.

Greater spearwort (*Ranunculus lingua*) Rare in the wild, but extremely invasive in 'captivity'. Tall stems up to 1.5 metres tall, with large leaves and topped by enormous buttercup flowers.

Flowering rush (*Butomus umbellatus*) Extremely beautiful.

Clusters of pretty pink/mauve flowers on a single stem, and tufts of slender, bright green leaves.

Burr reed (*Spargahium erectum*) Tough, sword-like leaves and spiky, globe-shaped fruits. The seed is particularly popular with birds.

Lesser reedmace (*Typha latifolia*) This is a rather slender, more elegant relative of the popular plant we generally call bullrush. Its big cousin. T. angustifolia) is really too invasive for garden ponds. Leave the seedheads to ripen and you will eventually see them ripped to bits by the sparrows.

This male broad-bodied darter was one of four spectacular species which bred in my pond in the very first year. Darters are territorial, and this one spent the whole of the early summer perched on its red-hot-poker, darting off occasionally to snap up a midge, to drive away a competitor, or to mate with a visiting female.

Birds must keep extra clean in winter, so that their feathers will fluff up properly, and keep them warm. Crowds of starlings, blackbirds and thrushes gather around my pond for mixed bathing parties on icy cold mornings.

made up of masses of water-snail eggs, and they are an absolute must if you hope to have a pond with clear water. If you don't inherit snails with your pond weed beg a few from a friend's pond, or buy a dozen from the pet shop. They soon multiply. Another way of introducing the more sedentary species of pond life is by transplanting a bucket or two of mud from some species-rich wetland. I scooped up half a bucket of black oozy slime from amongst the plants on the edge of a derelict canal I know, and poured it into my pond. As the black cloud mushroomed across the bottom of the pond, little wriggly creatures shot out in all directions. Some of them were almost certainly the damselfly larvae that emerged later that summer, climbed an inch or two up the base of the nearest flag iris, and emerged as iridescent blue fairytale insects, to dart around the pool margin, just above the water surface before coupling with a mate and performing amazing egg-laying gymnastics on the water lily leaves.

The water in a well balanced pond is a rich soup of tiny aquatic animals, all feeding either on rotting vegetation, even tinier green plants, or on one another. In a new pond, there is bound to be a shortage of dead plant material, and that can slow down development of the wildlife community. Researchers at the Game Conservancy's gravel pit laboratories near Milton Keynes have devised a clever way of solving this problem, and it is a technique which you might like to try in your new pond. Take an armful or two of clean straw, chop it into short lengths,

NATIVE WILDFLOWERS FOR THE POND

Plants which are floating-leaved and bottom-rooted

White waterlily (*Nymphaea alba*) This is a very vigorous native plant, capable of growing up in three metres of water, and producing large lily pads. It really is too big for normal garden ponds, though its flowers are very beautiful.

Yellow waterlily (*Nymphaea lutea*) Just as gigantic, but with simple yellow flowers, changing to strange bottle-shaped fruits.

Fringed waterlily (*Nymphoides peltata*) Available from garden centres, and much less aggressive. Delightful little single yellow flowers stand a few millimetres above the water surface and the circular leaves are about 75mm across.

Broad-leaved pond weed (*Potamogeton natans*) Lovely dark brown/green oval leaves lying flat on the surface. Insignificant flowers.

Amphibious bistort (*Polygonum amphibium*) One of the best pond plants, with oval floating leaves and pretty little pink flowers standing proud of the water. Snails lay their blobs of sticky eggs on the underside of the leaves and the seed is a popular food with several species.

Water crowfoot (*Ranunculus aquatilis*) Very pretty, simple white flowers and green, indented leaves about 30mm across. Flowers in early spring and disappears by mid-summer. The leaves below the surface are much more fern-like.

NATIVE WILDFLOWERS FOR
THE POND

Submerged aquatic plants – providing oxygen and cover for the more secretive pondlife.

Spiked water milfoil (*Myriophyllum spicatum*) Prefers 'hard water' and produces a mass of feathery green underwater stems. Flowers above the surface.

Curly pondweed (*Potamogeton crispus*) Crinkly leaves all the way along the stem and modest little flowers held just above the water surface.

Hornwort (*Ceratophyllum*

demersum) A solid-looking plant with much-branched stem. Very brittle but easy to anchor again.

Water starwort (*Callitriche* Spp) Delicate-looking pale-green plants which can cope with seasonal drought.

Canadian pondweed (*Elodea canadensis*) The most common 'oxygenator' in the garden centres, but *very* aggressive and difficult to contain. Very good if you have lots of deep water to keep it under control.

and float them out across the pond surface. This looks ridiculous, but after a day or two the straw will all have sunk to the bottom, and you will see a quite dramatic increase in invertebrate activity.

Frogs, toads and newts all depend on ponds for breeding. They spend the winter hibernating under logs, stones or other moist, safe places, and most of the summer wandering around in the long grass and moist vegetation hunting for slugs and small insects. In the spring, though, they return to their home pond, where they mate and the females lay their spawn. Most people are familiar with frogspawn, which comes in big blobs of spotty jelly, but toadspawn is laid as long double strands of eggs which sink to the bottom and wrap around the pondweed, and female newts stick their eggs to individual underwater leaves. Because of the strong homing instinct, there is little point trying to establish a breeding colony of amphibians by transplanting adults. That is cruel and in the case of some species it is actually a serious offence. It is worth transferring the spawn, though. Collect it when it is really fresh, and try only to remove it from a pond which is overpopulated, or where the misguided owners are 'anti-frog'. In very small ponds people often supplement the tadpoles' diet with a little catfood, but if the pond is well established, with plenty of resident plant and animal life, there shouldn't be any need to feed them.

It isn't a very good idea to have goldfish in a wildlife pond. Certainly you should never introduce frogspawn or tadpoles along with goldfish. The fish will eat them. Mind you, the frogs, or at least the toads, do sometimes get their own back. I have had several very upset goldfish fanciers complain to me that a passionate love-sick male toad, desperate to wrap its arms and legs around anything resembling a fertile female, has seized one of the prize *koi* carp and hugged it to death. I must say I find the newts that live in my pond infinitely more fascinating than fish, and certainly more needful of habitat help. However, if you are keen to introduce a fish or two, I suggest you go for sticklebacks if the pond is reasonably big, and perhaps a small tench or two to help vacuum clean the debris in the murky depths, if you have an angler friend who can come up with the goods.

One problem with artificial garden wetlands is that they have a nasty habit of losing water by evaporation in hot dry weather. The problem is worse in a wildlife wetland because all the plants that you have growing with their roots in the water act as a collection of very efficient wicks, and pump out the water even faster than normal. If you can collect the rainwater from the house roof, all well and good, though you will obviously need to store quite a lot. The drought problem can't really be solved otherwise, since of course there won't be any rain coming gushing down the drainpipe in the periods when you actually need it.

For one reason or another, though, you are likely to finish up putting in the hose pipe and turning on the tap. This can lead to problems. Most tap water these days is high in nutrients. In the big cities it may have been through at least one other pair of kidneys before it reaches you (via another purification plant of course) and some of the surplus artificial fertilisers we pour on the land inevitably find their way into the waterways eventually. When you add nutrient-rich water to the pond, you can find that you stimulate the growth of green slime. This 'algal bloom' is a perfectly natural response to extra fertility, but it doesn't look very good, it can lock up the oxygen which the pond species need, and if it gets really bad, it can cut out the light too. There are chemicals available which kill 'blanket weed', but please don't be tempted to use them. They don't solve the cause of the problem, they just obscure the effect for a while. Rake out the green slime if it gets really bad, and put it on the compost heap. Take out some of the other vegetation towards the end of the summer too. That will help to reduce the nutrient surplus in the pond. The best advice, though, seems to be to leave well alone, and let nature take a hand. I had very thick green blanket weed in my new pond the first year. I raked quite a lot of it out, but the second year there was a boom in the snail population. These amazing creatures sucked and munched their way casually around the pond, sweeping up any spare bit of algae that floated by, and the water remained crystal clear, despite top-ups from the tap and an exceptionally sunny summer. The golden rule with wildlife gardening and habitat management seems to be "If in doubt, leave it alone." It is remarkable how often nature finds a way of sorting the problem out and restoring a healthy balance.

PART 3

Supplementing the Habitats

Chapter 8

Cottage garden service station

THE GARDEN can be a richer habitat than anything you might find in nature. Although the size eventually puts a limit on the number and variety of species you can actually have *living* with you, it is possible to boost the habitat, and develop your garden as a very attractive service station for extra, passing wildlife. Your pond will tend to serve as quite a magnet anyway, with flocks of birds and a stream of small mammals visiting it to drink, but moving on elsewhere to breed. One of the joys of calm summer evenings in my wildlife garden is the bats. A pair, sometimes three, arrive every night at dusk, and fly silently round and round the pond, about a metre above the surface. They are presumably sweeping up the last few unsuspecting midges that have hatched during the day, but they generally swoop down and snatch a drink from the pool whilst they are there, too. I had always assumed that my bats were pipistrelles. They are the most common town bats, although like all their relatives they are declining in numbers at a very worrying rate. Their problems arise largely from all the spraying that now goes on in roof cavities. I recently had a 'bat expert' visiting the garden, who felt my bats might be a rather less common species called natterers bat. To be honest, I don't much mind whether the wildlife in my garden is rare or common. The sight of these visitors flitting across the moon is thrilling, and since even the tiny pipistrelle is capable of gobbling up 3,500 insects in a night, they are helping to reduce the chances of any of those midges and mosquitoes biting me. The point is that, so far as I know, my bats don't live here. They simply visit on a regular basis because they like the menu at my service station. Without the pond and its midges they would probably still fly over from time to time, but they wouldn't come right down low, where I can watch them perform.

The most important feature of any service station, wildlife or otherwise, is the food and drink, and this is where you can really score if you know what you are doing. Native plants are critical for a balanced, ecologically sound wildlife community, but many of the more mobile and spectacular creatures, particularly insects such as butterflies and moths, and the songbirds, feed mainly on nectar, pollen or seed. You can give a tremendous boost to their larder by planting colourful flowery 'cottage garden' style borders, and I strongly recommend that you concentrate them near the house. This policy has two advantages. It brings the butterflies and birds very close to your windows, and it provides an

---

GARDEN BORDER FLOWERS FOR NECTAR AND/OR SEED.

Listed in approximate order of flowering – January to December

Christmas Rose (*Helleborus niger*)
Winter aconite (*Eranthis hyemalis*)
Elephant's ears (*Bergenia cordifolia*)
Spring crocus (*Crocus chrysanthus and hybrids*)
Anemone (*Anemone blanda*)
Grape hyacinth (*Muscari botryoides*)
Lenten rose (*Helleborus orientalis*)
Polyanthus (*Primula vulgaris elatior*)
Soldiers and sailors (*Pulmonaria saccharata*)
White arabis (single) (*Arabis albida*)
Honesty (*Lunaria biennis*)
Sweet rocket (*Hesperis matronalis*)
Aubretia (*Aubretia deltoides*)
Wallflowers (*Cheiranthus cheiri*)
Forget-me-not (*Myosotis* spp)
Leopard's-bane (*Doronicum pardalianches*)
Golden alyssum (*Alyssum saxatile*)
Sweet William (*Dianthus barbatus*)
Perennial cornflower (*Centaurea*)
Poached egg plant (*Limnanthes douglasii*)
Shasta daisy (*Chrysanthemum maximum*)
Fleabane (*Erigeron speciosus* varieties)
Cranesbills (*Geranium* species)
Sweet bergamot (*Monarda didyma*)
Evening primrose (*Oenothera biennis*)
Oriental poppy (*Papaver orientale*)
Spiked speedwell (*Veronica spicata*)
Valerian (*Centranthus ruber*)

Sweet alyssum (*Lobularia maritima*)
Angelica (*Angelica archangelica*)
Lovage (*Levesticum officinale*)
Tobacco plant (*Nicotiana affinis*)
Mignonette (*Reseda odorata*)
Corncockle (*Agrostemma githago*)
Yarrow (*Achillea filipendulina*)
Alkanet (*Anchusa azurea*)
Chicory (*Cichorium intybus*)
Yellow loosestrife (*Lysimachia vulgaris*)
Hollyhock (*Alcea rosea*)
Snapdragon (*Antirrhinum majus*)
Candytuft (*Iberis umbellata*)
Californian poppy (*Eschscholtzia californica*)
Sunflower (*Helianthus annuus*)
Mallow (*Lavatera rosea*)
Golden rod (*Solidago canadensis*)
Phlox (*Phlox paniculata*)
Teasel (*Dipsacus fullonum*)
Basil (*Ocimum basilicum*)
Mint (*Mentha rotundifolia*)
Globe thistle (*Echinops ritro*)
Meadow saffron (*Colchicum autumnale*)
Cosmos (*Cosmea bipinnatus*)
Cherry pie (*Heliotropum x hybridum*)
Michaelmas daisy (*Aster amellus, A. acris., A. novae angliae, A. novi belgii*)
Ice plant (*Sedum spectabile*)

NOTE: Many of these plants will flower in autumn if you cut off some of their dead summer flowers. Don't forget to leave some to seed.

Some of our native
wildflowers are well worth a
place in the service station
flower garden. This is yellow
toadflax, (*Linaria vulgaris*), a
common enough weed of
railway embankments and
waste ground which
flourishes under cultivation,
and flowers in late summer.

These flowers are growing in
a seed nursery run by a friend
in north Holland. Almost all
of them are native
wildflowers, and this shows
just how spectacularly
colourful these valuable
plants can be.

'orthodox' landscape around the buildings, emphasising the more relaxed 'countryside' atmosphere in the rest of the wildlife garden.

The ideal 'larder border' is a mixture of flowering and fruiting shrubs, herbaceous perennials and colourful seasonal bedding. Your aim should be to provide a source of 'natural' food for as long a period of each year as possible, and that means starting in very early spring with some of the garden bulbs, and leaving herbaceous plants to run to seed as an attraction to finches in particular in the very late autumn. There are lots of books around which discuss mixed borders. The idea really began at

NATIVE WILDFLOWERS FOR THE FLOWER BORDER

I have grouped these according to colour, to make them easier to design with.

Mauve, purple and pink

Greater knapweed (*Centaurea scabiosa*). Thistle-like flowerheads the size of a shaving brush. Flowers in July. Popular with butterflies. Height 600mm.

Hardhead (*Centaurea nigra*) Similar to greater knapweed but smaller flowers.

Spear thistle (*Cirsium vulgare*) Elegant thistle 1.5m tall. Purple flowerheads all summer. Popular with butterflies. Clouds of fluffy seed-heads attract finches in early autumn.

Lesser Burdock (*Arctium minus*) A coarse biennial up to 2 metres high that seeds readily. Flowers attract butterflies, goldfinches feed on seeds, and the 'burrs' fix to clothes for ease of transport.

Hemp agrimony (*Eupatorium cannabinum*) Beautiful wetland perennial with plates of flowers in July, up to 1.5m tall. Excellent butterfly plant.

Teasel (*Dipsacus fullonum*) One of the best 'service-station' wildflowers. Two metres tall and statuesque in form. Birds drink from the rainwater trapped in leaf-forks, bees and butterflies queue up for the pink pollen in August, and goldfinches find the seeds irresistible.

Field scabious (*Knautia arvensis*) Very pretty perennial which flowers all summer. Particularly popular with crimson burnet moths and soldier beetles.

Foxglove (*Digitalis purpurea*) Biennial, so it must be allowed to colonise. Seedlings need thinning for the best display. Tall, beautiful spikes of richly-marked 'thimble' flowers constantly visited by bumblebees in June.

Woody nightshade (*Solanum dulcamara*) Poisonous, but well worth a safe place in the hedgerow or amongst shrubs. Scrambling growth, clusters of striking mauve and yellow flowers, followed by bunches of orange and scarlet berries.

Wild thyme (*Thymus serpyllum*) Very low-growing, aromatic herb. Covered in mauve flowers through June and July, and crawling with bees and butterflies. Needs a sunny, welldrained, slightly limy position to do well.

Marjoram (*Origanum vulgare*) Another aromatic culinary herb, this time growing 300–500mm tall. Tolerates very poor soil and full sun.

Betony (*Stachys officinalis*) A classic bee-plant, flowering in mid-summer.

Hedge-woundwort (*Stachys sylvatica*) Shade-tolerant, with 600mm spikes of 'snap-dragon-like' little flowers arranged in tiers. Popular the end of the last century, when they were championed by the great garden writers William Robinson and Gertrude Jekyll. My great hero of modern day planting design is Christopher Lloyd. His border at Great Dixter must be a dream come true for the local bees and butterflies, and my own little flower borders owe a great deal to his ideas.

There are actually quite a lot of native plants which are more than a match for the flamboyant herbaceous hybrids. Some of them are fantastic wildlife attractors, and I strongly recommend them. There are quite a few plants too, which began life as garden flowers, escaped into the

with the smaller species of bees.

Red deadnettle (*Lamium purpureum*) A carpeting plant with beautifully marked green and white leaves. Flowers throughout the year. A good, shade-tolerant bee-plant up to 200mm tall.

Thrift (*Armeria maritima*) A grass-like plant of cliff-tops, often grown in rockeries. Must have acid soil, but is then an excellent late-summer source of nectar. The evergreen tussocks provide good shelter for wildlife.

Purple loose-strife (*Lythrum salicaria*) A tall marsh-plant with spectacular spikes of flowers up to 2 metres tall. Popular with butterflies and bees.

Rosebay willow-herb (*Epilobium angustifolium*) Treat with caution. This is a most spectacular plant, with beautiful tall spikes of cerise flowers in July and August. Bees love it, and the leaves feed the caterpillar of elephant hawkmoth, but it is very invasive, and produces clouds of fluffy seeds each year. Grow a clump in a tub (where it can't spread) and cut off the flower-stems at the first sign of seeding.

Musk mallow (*Malva sylvestris*) One of the prettiest of the taller wildflowers. A loose, branching habit up to 2 metres tall, with large, open flowers.

Herb robert (*Geranium robertianum*) One of my favourite wildflowers. The whole plant is tinged with red, and the little 'cranesbill'

flowers put on a pretty display throughout the summer. Grows happily in cracks in paving and walls, and along the hedge-bottom.

Wood cranesbill (*Geranium sylvaticum*) Shade-tolerant as the name suggests, with deep mauve flowers in mid-summer, and lush herbaceous growth to 600mm.

Sainfoin (*Onobrychis viciifolia*) One of the 'pea' family tolerates poor soil but prefers slightly limy soil.

Night-flowering catchfly (*Silene noctiflora*) An interesting plant. Pretty little flowers in July and August, and the stems and leaves are sticky. It flowers at night, with a super perfume. Excellent moth plant.

Corncockle (*Agrostemma githago*) Perhaps the most elegant of all our cornfield 'weeds'. An annual with open habit, and cerise flowers held on stems up to 1 metre tall. Provides colour all summer, and produces large black seeds which fall to the ground and germinate the following spring.

Soapwort (*Saponaria officinalis*) Masses of pink, phlox-like flowers, 75mm tall; flowers in August and September. It has a delicate scent which attracts hawkmoths, and the fresh green leaves can be boiled to produce a soap substitute.

Red campion (*Silene dioica*) An easy and very beautiful wildflower to grow. Woodland-edge and hedgebottom its preferred habitat. 600mm tall. Flowers in May and again in September or October.

countryside years ago, and are now classified as 'wildflowers', so the situation is rather confused anyway. I will leave you to consult the panels in this chapter for a full choice of service station species, but there are one or two particular 'stars' which I think are worth a special mention. Top of the charts for me is the teasel. This is a biennial, which means you have to sow seed for two consecutive springs if you want flowers every year. (I mentioned this earlier in connection with foxgloves.) Once you have teasels established, though, you will never be short of them provided you allow a few seedlings to survive each year. They are very good at colonising. The plant itself is exceptionally handsome. It grows as a flat rosette in the first year, and the cartwheel of leaves is covered in short, knobbly spines. In the second spring your teasels will rumble into life in April, and shoot up to over two metres in height in a matter of a month or so, producing a perfectly symmetrical flower stem of paired side shoots as elegant as any candelabra. In the angle of each side shoot there is a large, water-tight pocket, formed by fused bracts wrapped around the stem, and this is the first wildlife feature. Rainwater collects in these little reservoirs, and you will almost certainly see sparrows drinking there by late spring. The water also seems to trap a surprising number of small insects, and there is some discussion as to whether teasels might be slightly carnivorous. The teasel flowers generally come out in mid-July. The flowerhead is the size and shape of an upturned egg cup, covered in soft green bristles at this stage, and the flowers open just like a mauve belt around the middle. This first band of miniature blossoms lasts a day or two, and as it fades, a pair of replacement rings opens, one above and one below. As the week goes by, the two bands of flowers move wider and wider apart, until all the flowers have been pollinated and the performance is over. The colour of the teasel pollen is deep lavender/pink, and there is a great deal of it. Big bumblebees seem to be the main pollinators, and they look like rather overweight punk-rocker 'wall of death' riders as they crawl horizontally around each belt of flowers, covering themselves with pink pollen. The flowers are also popular with summer butterflies, and the ones in my garden often seem to attract the small species such as common skipper, common blue and small copper. Blue butterflies on pink flowers are particularly pretty.

Once the teasel flowers have been pollinated and the seed begins to form, the whole of the flowerhead hardens, and turns to a rich brown colour. The bristles stiffen, and even nowadays there are teasels grown commercially, particularly in Somerset, for use in the weaving mills of Yorkshire. Long rows of dried teasel heads are used to 'fluff up' the surface of the very best worsted. If you look closely at the brown seedheads you will see a densely packed honeycomb of little chambers, each one containing a large brown seed. Some of these will be shaken out by the wind, and a few will germinate to produce next year's seedlings.

The vast majority, though, never stand a chance. Teasels are particularly popular with goldfinches. They seem to know instinctively when to begin visiting the seedheads, and there really is no more colourful sight on a frosty winter's morning, than a charm of these cheerful little birds with their black and yellow wings and their brilliant crimson faces, fluttering

NATIVE WILDFLOWERS FOR THE FLOWER BORDER

Blue

Meadow cranesbill (*Geranium pratense*) A low, spreading herbaceous perennial, 450mm tall, preferring limy soils. Popular with bees.

Bluebell (*Endymion non-scriptus*) Plant as bulbs. Seedlings take several years to reach flowering size. Wonderful perfume on still, damp days. Grows best in the shade of deciduous shrubs and trees.

Chicory (*Cichorium intybus*) Startling blue flowers for four months through the summer. Flower stems well over 2 metres tall, and a constant source of 'bee' activity.

Cornflower (*Centaurea cyanus*) An annual, now available in a whole range of colours. Grow the native cornflower blue type mixed in with poppies and corn marigold for a spectacular summer display.

Great bellflower (*Campanula latifolia*) Sturdy flower-stem up to 1 metre tall, covered in large flowers. Best in moist soil and half-shade.

Nettle-leaved bellflower (*Campanula trachelium*) Similar to above.

Harebell (*Campanula rotundifolia*) A favourite wildflower. Tough, wiry stems and the most delicate of bell-like flowers. It grows wild amongst dwarf grasses in acid soils, but thrives in the kinder conditions of a flower-border, so long as the soil is not too limy.

Clustered bellflower (*Campanula glomerata*) Similar to C. *latifolia*, but with a bunch of bell-flowers at the tip of each stem.

Devil's bit scabious (*Succisa pratensis*) Week after week of pretty blue flowers, nodding about 600mm above the leaves. Food plant for the caterpillars of marsh fritillary butterflies.

Germander speedwell (*Veronica chamaedrys*) Invasive, but not overwhelming. A very pretty ground-cover with sheets of flowers in May. Important for early foraging bees.

Self-heal (*Prunella vulgaris*) A lawn weed that is transformed by cultivation. Deep purple/blue flowers up to 100mm tall, above a carpet of deep-green leaves. Good groundcover and a useful bee-plant.

Bugle (*Ajuga reptans*) Lots of garden varieties, some with variegated leaves. Prefers shade and moisture. Spikes of flowers up to 150mm tall in May and June.

Viper's bugloss (*Echium vulgare*) One of the best wild flowers for hot, dry gravelly soils. Friends of mine have it naturalised all over their gravel drive. Flower spikes up to 1 metre tall, all summer long.

Green alkanet (*Pentaglottis sempervirens*) Another dazzling blue flower. Grow it amongst the nettles in a damp, shady corner, or give it pride of place in the flower border. Over 1 metre tall in mid-summer.

Wood forget-me-not (*Myosotis sylvatica*) More delicate than the highly refined garden varieties. Very beautiful, shade-tolerant and flowers for months on end.

around the tips of the teasels, chattering musically to one another as they tease out seed after seed.

There are several other tall biennials that are worth including at the back of your borders. The giant mullein (*Verbascum bombycifera*) has huge hairy grey leaves at ground level, and a spike of yellow and brown flowers over two metres tall in its second season. It produces tens of thousands of tiny seeds, and its leaves are the food plant for a particularly spectacular caterpillar – the mullein moth.

Angelica is another big biennial which I love to grow. There is a native species, but the herb-garden variety is bigger and even more dramatic. The fresh, green leaves are wonderful as a foliage display, and the huge bunches of tiny green flowers buzz above your head, attracting dozens of hoverflies and bees. In autumn the dry, brown flower-stems are topped by a mass of big golden seeds, visited by greenfinches and bluetits.

NATIVE WILDFLOWERS FOR THE FLOWER BORDER

Yellow

Rough hawkbit (*Leontodon hispidus*) One of the tallest of the 'dandelion' types. Extremely handsome, and a very long summer flowering season, but you must control the seedlings.

Yellow toadflax (*Linaria vulgaris*) A must in the wildlife garden. One of the loveliest of wildflowers, flowering late into the autumn and growing on any soil. A bee plant.

Ragwort (*Senecio jacobaea*) A 'notifiable' weed in the farming countryside, because its leaves taint the milk when cows eat them. Pretty, daisy-like flowers, and the leaves are food for the caterpillars of cinnabar moths.

Corn marigold (*Chrysanthemum segetum*) A very pretty annual. Grow it just like Californian poppies or calendulas.

Ox-eye daisy (*Leucanthemum vulgare*) Meadow flowers which can be cultivated to produce lovely cut-flowers, just like giant daisies.

Common fleabane (*Pulicaria dysenterica*) A rich orange-yellow daisy-flower about 600mm tall.

Tansy (*Tanacetum vulgare*) Aromatic leaves (used for flavouring sponge cakes) and button-like flowers oozing with nectar in July. Hoverflies and small butterflies are constant visitors. The plant spreads by underground stems, and can be invasive.

Yellow archangel (*Lamiastrum galeobdolon*) A woodland plant with spikes of very beautiful 'bee' flowers from early spring onwards.

Cowslip (*Primula veris*) Prefers lime, but once your clumps are established they will flower for years, and can be split from time to time – just like polyanthus. Cowslips hybridise very easily, and you may have seedlings with bronze flowers appearing after a year or two of promiscuous suburban life.

Oxlip (*Primula elatior*) Like a bunch of primroses on a stem. A woodland plant with a lovely pale cream colour. Looks wonderful flowering amongst violets in early spring.

Primrose (*Primula vulgaris*) Grows best in half-shade, particularly on sandy soil with a covering of fallen leaves. If you have the patience to

COTTAGE GARDEN SERVICE STATION

One more biennial is worth a special mention. This is the evening primrose (*Oenothera biennis*). Again it can be a little over-enthusiastic in its colonising, but there is no better flower for attracting night-flying moths, and the pure primrose yellow of its metre and a half tall blooms is lovely. Flowers open each evening, just before sunset, and each one lasts until noon the following day. The perfume at night is wonderful, and if you care to venture out after dark you will find the evening primroses lighting up your garden, and playing larder to a jostling cloud of moths. I understand that the oil contained in evening primrose seed is proving to be very special – the only kind that doesn't aggravate heart disease in humans, apparently. I read somewhere that the crushed seed might be a healthy addition to my morning muesli, and that evening primrose is likely to be the next boom crop of British agriculture. That should certainly please the moths, just so long as the farmers leave them the odd

dead-head, primroses will flower almost the whole year round. The leaves are often patterned by the tunnels of leaf-miners and ants feed on the waxy coating of primrose seed.

Rockrose (*Helianthemum nummularium*) A tiny native shrub of limestone grasslands. Evergreen, with lots of single and double garden varieties in all colours. The true native type is pure yellow, and flowers whenever the sun shines, from June to September.

Dyers wintergreen (*Genista tinctoria*) Similar to gorse, but smaller (1 metre tall) and without the prickles.

Tormentil (*Potentilla erecta*) Rare in the wild. An extremely pretty flower growing 600mm tall, and blooming in early summer.

Agrimony (*Agrimonia eupatoria*) An important medicinal herb, and also a useful dye plant, producing a rich yellow colour. The flowers are small, on spikes about 600mm tall. The leaves are similar to those of meadow sweet, and the fruit have hooks on them, and cling to your socks.

Stonecrop (*Sedum acre*) A tiny succulent, a bit like a cactus. Survives the toughest of conditions, produces a brilliant sheet of flowers in early summer, and the fleshy leaves turn red in dry periods.

Greater celandine (*Chelidonium majus*) One of my favourite wildflowers. The leaves are a particularly fresh green, the flowers are pretty too, and the plant will colonise open ground and thrive in the woodland-edge. The fruits split to reveal a row of shiny black seeds, each with a white blob on. This is a waxy material which ants feed on and in carrying off the seed they help with dispersal.

Globe flower (*Trollius europaeus*) This elegant plant looks too 'posh' to be a wildflower. Like a giant buttercup with spherical blooms, it grows naturally in wet ground, but seems happy in most garden conditions. There are various shades of yellow and orange available, but I still prefer the simple butter-yellow of the native type.

Welsh poppy (*Meconopsis cambrica*) Not native to most of the British Isles of course, but so lovely it should be in everyone's garden. It grows best as an annual, seeding merrily into cracks and crevices, but the odd plant may survive for two or three years.

NATIVE WILDFLOWERS FOR THE FLOWER BORDER

Green

Stinking hellebore (*Helleborus foetidus*) A dramatic, rather sinister plant of chalk woodlands. Very strong leaf-shape, dark leathery green leaves, and clusters of handsome green flowers, each with a purple margin. The seed pods produce an acrid smell if you crush them. Flowers appear as early as February, and are a useful souce of nectar for newly-emerged bees.

Lady's mantle (*Alchemilla vulgaris*) A perennial which seeds readily into paved areas. The green flowers come in 'clouds' in mid-summer, and the leaves are extremely pretty, often holding a droplet of water in the centre, and always looking fresh.

wild corner, too, full of native plants on which they can lay their eggs. Evening primrose originates in North America, but you can find it growing wild on poor, gravelly soils all over Europe.

When it comes to choosing service station flowers, probably the best advice I can offer is for you to keep your eyes open in other people's gardens. You will quickly spot the plants which seem to be attracting all the butterflies, or providing the favourite seed for small birds. Generally speaking, it seems best to avoid frilly double varieties. Many of these are so over-bred that they no longer produce pollen, nectar or seed, poor things, and so they may as well be plastic for all the use wildlife can make of them.

Mauve and purple flowers seem to be particularly popular with butterflies, and hoverflies prefer the yellows and golds. Some flowers are very specifically designed for a particular type of pollinator. Snapdragons and broad beans, for instance, simply won't open up for anything lighter than a substantial bumblebee.

Try to choose flowers which will turn into useful seedheads wherever possible, and remember you will be particularly popular with the wildlife if you can provide nectar very early and very late in the season. My service station opens for business in late January, when a couple of days of unexpected sunshine bring out the little yellow flowers of winter aconite. Any insect that happens to have been caught in a warming sunbeam and stirred into activity must be very glad to find my garden. After the aconites come the snowdrops, but to be honest not many insects seem to be able to manage the gymnastics involved in tapping their pendulous little flowers.

Grape hyacinth is much more convenient. It seeds itself in ever-increasing numbers under my apple tree, and on one warm day very early last spring I watched a small tortoiseshell, a brimstone and two peacock butterflies working their way from flower to flower, dipping into the nectar and no doubt helping with pollination at the same time. The early

OPPOSITE: The apple tree is just one of the many garden plants which provides a boost to passing wildlife in my cottage garden service station.

122

crocuses are valuable, too. Their flowers are generally too deep for the butterflies to take advantage of, except on those occasional bright, sunny days when the petals fold right back, but the first bees to emerge after the winter certainly make good use of the crocus pollen. Plant the ordinary yellow crocus and you will probably be entertained (or annoyed) by the local sparrow gang too. It is remarkable how they seem to love ripping these innocent little flowers to bits. It looks like hooliganism, but presumably they're really after the high protein pollen.

Another early spring flower which I think symbolises the cottage garden is honesty (*Lunaria biennis*). Coincidentally, this is yet another biennial, and again it happily colonises the cracks in the paving slabs, or any other soil pockets it can find. Its flowers are a shade of purple which would be quite vulgar at any other time of year, but in early spring, when there is little else in flower, a patch of honesty flowers is a real source of delight. Butterflies love honesty flowers. The early orange-tips are particularly attracted to them, and this plant has become an alternative to the native lady's smock and garlic mustard as the food plant for their caterpillars. As the honesty finishes, its place is taken by sweet rocket – yet another biennial which this time provides hundreds of sweetly-

NATIVE WILDFLOWERS FOR THE FLOWER BORDER

White

White deadnettle (*Lamium album*) A marvellous bee-plant and a good groundcover plant. Spreads by seed and runner.

White campion (*Silene alba*) Crops up as an annual in weedy cornfields, but you can grow it for several years in the flower border. Purest white flowers, up to 750mm tall.

Scentless Mayweed (*Matricaria maritima*) A cornfield wildflower. Grow it mixed with poppies and cornflowers.

Sneezewort (*Achillea ptarmica*) A rich source of nectar in late summer. Fern-like, feathery leaves but it can become over-invasive. Height 300–400mm.

Sanicle (*Sanicula europaea*) Tiny white flowers, but very shade-tolerant and delicate-looking.

Masterwort (*Astrantia major*) This is a lovely plant, with delicate, jewel-like flower heads from May onwards. Shade-tolerant and 600mm tall.

Seakale (*Crambe maritima*) A dramatic perennial, producing clouds of flowers smelling sweetly of honey. The cabbage-like leaves are very handsome too, and the whole plant is quite spectacular in June.

Jack-by-the-hedge (*Alliaria petiolata*) An early spring flower, growing as a biennial with a tough rootstock. It seeds readily, is shade tolerant and its leaves are used as a food plant by the caterpillars of orange-tip butterflies.

Bladder-campion (*Silene vulgaris*) Similar to white campion but not so tall (300mm).

Greater stitchwort (*Stellaria holostea*) Very pretty star-like flowers throughout the summer – but the plant can be very invasive.

scented, white or pale pink flowers, and again orange-tip caterpillars can eat the leaves. Honesty is one of those bonus plants which also produces useful seed. The translucent 'silver pennies' are much loved by flower arrangers, but mine stay firmly on the plants until the last one has been eaten. Bullfinches seem to be remarkably good at tackling these big, papery fruits. They crouch on the ground and then leap up, fluttering their wings frantically, and grab a 'silver penny' in their beak. Their reward is two or three big brown seeds, and they have no difficulty at all ripping off the packaging once they are back on the ground.

At the other end of the year, Michaelmas daisies are probably the border flowers that provide the latest heavy crop of nectar. This is most important for those species of insects which overwinter as adults. They need to build up their energy store before retiring for the duration, and that is why Michaelmas daisies are so popular with the small tortoise-shells and brimstones. Some of the Michaelmas daisies produce a very good seed crop after they have flowered. The species tend to be rather more fruitful than the larger flowered hybrids, so it is worth bearing this in mind when choosing.

Michaelmas daisies are just the last in a long line of very good nectar and pollen plants you might like to grow. Some of them seem to prompt very amusing antics from their pollinators. I grow the large-flowered border poppies, for instance, because I love to watch the bees crawling on their sides, and wallowing in the black pollen. They adopt the same position with several other very open flowers. Pink mallow is a favourite, growing three metres tall, and filling the border with colour from late July onwards, and our own native cranesbill (*Geranium pratense*) is a lovely bee plant for the front of the border. There are dozens of garden cranesbills, too, all of them attractive to bees, and quite a lot of them produce a good seed crop. Ripe cranesbill fruits are especially beautiful. The panels of the 'beak' peel off from the 'wrong end' to form a five-pointed crown, with the tip of each curved arm decorated by a loosely dangling seed at the outer tip. Again the bullfinches in particular seem to go for them.

Several herbaceous perennials are worth growing especially for their seed. Achillea, for instance, is very showy in mid-summer, with its flat plates of tiny yellow flowers, and the hoverflies seem to enjoy the nectar, but if you leave the flower stems to ripen they will produce really tough seedheads, capable of supporting crowds of sparrows, greenfinches and tits. Golden rod (*Solidago canadensis*) is another border plant that is good for seed. It is very invasive, and you will need to keep controlling the size of the clumps, but the great plumes of yellow flowers in August and September are constantly alive with insects, and there must be ten thousand or more fluffy seeds on every stem by the autumn. Globe thistle (*Echinops ritro*), chicory (*Cichorium intybus*), globe artichoke (*Cynara scolymus*), rose campion (*Lychnis coronaria*) and many more produce really good seed crops if you let them, so don't chop off all the dead heads the minute the flowers have faded. You are missing a treat if you do. Goldfinches and bullfinches are far and away the most colourful display you could ever wish for in a *winter* flower border.

The herb garden is a very rich source of inspiration for the wildlife gardener. A great many of our culinary herbs produce pollen-rich flowers, and some of them have good seedheads, too. I mentioned angelica earlier, and two of the best of all herbs for insects are quite close relatives. One is lovage, which looks very similar indeed, but has flatter, smaller flowerheads, and the other is fennel, a beautiful plant with feathery, green or bronze leaves and a yellow umbel of flowers very like those of lovage. Incidentally, the leaves of both lovage and fennel are delicious for flavouring chicken and fish respectively. Both these umbellifers (the posh name for the cow-parsley family) are perennials, and both are quite well-behaved, so I suggest you plant them as a feature of some sunny border close to the kitchen door. They grow very tall – at least two metres by mid-summer, but they are both quite slender plants and don't take up a great deal of room otherwise. When the flowers are open, you can actually see the droplets of nectar, temptingly displayed to lure passing pollinators, and generally there is a whole collection of different hoverflies, wasps and bees staggering around in the sweet stickiness.

Try to provide nectar and pollen from very early spring to late autumn. Anemone blanda and grape hyacinth (*Muscari botryoides*) are two of the earliest garden plants to flower and can be a life-saver for precocious over-wintering butterflies.

Keep your eyes open for good wildlife plants. This is globe thistle (*Echinops ritro*) and it obviously appeals to bumblebees.

At a slightly lower level, chicory deserves to be grown more often. Its value in the kitchen lies in the roots, which can be dried and ground as a rather unconvincing substitute for coffee, but it produces a wonderful display of sky blue flowers all through the summer, stands a metre and a half high, and follows its flowers with a useful crop of early accessible bird-seed. No one seems very sure whether or not chicory is a native, but it can be found growing on wasteland and by the roadside, particularly in southern England. If you stumble across it in combination with evening primroses, the effect can be quite stunning. Their flowers only actually overlap for about four hours each day, because chicory opens in the early morning, and both plants have lost their colour by mid-day.

At the ground-hugging level in the herb garden, there are lots of really useful insect plants. Chives, for instance, produce their pretty purple balls of flower in June, and are visited by bees from morning till night. I like to grow them alongside cranebills, some of which have a flower of exactly the same colour.

Tansy is a native herb which I grow for the flavour of its deep green leaves, and for the butterflies attracted to its little yellow button flowers. Every summer, throughout the month of August, my tansy clump seems to be adopted by one particularly loyal small-copper butterfly, which just spends every hour of every day working its way backwards and forwards over the flowers. Rosemary flowers are good for bees, and lavender is

Sedum spectabile is a valuable butterfly plant. Its flowers provide nectar long after most garden flowers have run to seed. Here it is backed by the last of the flowers on my nicotiana.

very popular with butterflies. One of the best bee plants of all is borage, a handsome plant which grows very easily from seed. It has piercing blue flowers which hang down in bunches, and the bees queue up for a delicious, upside-down drink of the nectar. Borage flowers are the traditional decoration for gin and tonic, so there is a chance for you to join the intoxicated bees, too.

Parsley is a herb that we grow for its leaves, and normally it isn't encouraged to flower. If you do give it its head, though, and this sometimes happens if the weather is very dry and you are away for a couple of weeks, then you will find another of those umbelliferous green flowers decorating your herb border. If you want to guarantee a flower crop, then protect the parsley over winter and it will flower like mad in its second year. Quite a lot of insects seem to enjoy parsley flowers, but one in particular, the soldier beetle, seems to turn up as if by magic, and all through the early summer you will see the handsome chestnut-coloured creatures wandering over the flowers, more often than not locked together in mating tandem.

Mint, marjoram and lemon balm are three more leaf herbs that you should encourage to flower. Mint in particular is one of the very best butterfly plants there is – almost as compulsive as buddleia, and it really couldn't be easier to grow.

Talking of buddleia, there are one or two shrubs which give a specially useful boost to your wildlife service station. The famous butterfly bush is obvious. It really is incredible to see how many butterflies and bees manage to cling on to each spike of perfumed flowers. The common mauve seedlings that have colonised so many of our inner-city demolition sites seem at least as popular as the more sophisticated white, deep purple or red named hybrids, and there are less common species of Buddleia, too. *B. sellowiana* and *B. globosa*, for instance, have yellow flowers but that doesn't seem to bother the butterflies.

Flowering currant is another plant that is worth growing. I inherited a couple of big specimens in my garden, and was delighted to find that they were really good for bees. The tassels of pink flowers come out very early – usually before the end of May, and at that time of year these are probably the richest source of pollen and nectar in the garden. I've noticed that the bluetits spend a lot of time in the bushes, too, but I cannot quite work out whether they are after the nectar in the flowers, or the aphids and insect eggs around the base of the leaves. Lilac and mock orange are both very rich in nectar, but they only flower for a very short time. A number of the garden viburnums are very useful since they flower as early as January in some years, and the native viburnums, lantana and opulus, are quite showy enough for the border. The oriental privet is a good insect shrub if it is allowed to flower, though you do need a lot of space for that to happen. I used to love the sweet smell of white privet

EXOTIC SHRUBS FOR NECTAR, POLLEN OR FRUITS

Pyracantha coccinea White flowers in spring and orange or red berries. Blackbirds enjoy the fruit. Train it against a wall.

Cotoneaster frigida A semi-evergreen erect shrub, growing 2 metres tall, and useful as an informal hedge. Lots of berries in the autumn.

Cotoneaster horizontalis Deciduous and prostrate habit. Fantastic for bees, which cover the shrub when it flowers in early spring.

Viburnum bodnantense Flowers with a delicious perfume in January and February. Useful for the time of year.

Chaenomeles japonica Japanese quince. Red flowers before the leaves come out, and large apple-like fruit which the thrushes, starlings and blackbirds enjoy once they fall in autumn.

Amelanchier canadensis Lovely autumn colour and masses of white blossom in March and April.

Viburnum tinus Evergreen, grows 2 to 3 metres tall and flowers through the winter. Very useful as a nectar source for hibernating insects that wake up by mistake.

Mahonia spp. The Oregon grape and others are useful evergreens, because they flower so early in the spring. Bees visit them for pollen, and *M. aquifolium* produces a good crop of purple berries in the autumn.

flowers when I played on the local derelict allotments as a child, and the great columns of black berries are valuable as winter food for birds.

Brooms are extremely good bee plants, and the native, *Cytisus scoparius*, is one of the best flowerers if you have room for it. Broom tends to be short-lived, and usually dies after six or seven years, but at its peak, in years four or five, it is a spectacular blaze of yellow in June. If you haven't room to accommodate a plant the size of a mature wild broom, then there are several more compact species. *Cytisus praecox* is particularly good and it flowers a little earlier too.

Shrub roses are perhaps some of the most useful of wildlife 'ornamental shrubs'. There is a whole range of very elegant species and modern varieties, some of them growing well over three metres tall, and they give a double benefit by producing plenty of pollen, particularly in the more simple flowers, and following on with big juicy hips in the autumn. Rose leaves are also the favourite building material used by leaf-cutter bees, which cut neat circles to cart away to their nest. The young rose shoots are popular with aphids, of course, and they in turn provide food for a range of insect predators.

A number of other garden shrubs are useful for their fruit crop. There is a whole range of berberis, cotoneasters and mahonias to choose from, and quite a number flower very early in the spring, when pollen and nectar are in short supply. Pyracantha I mentioned as a possible wall shrub, but it can be grown more freely if you prefer, and japonica, or

Californian poppies (*Eschscholtzia Californica*) are cheap and easy to grow from seed. Keep deadheading them and you will attract lots of different hoverflies right through the summer.

Chaenomeles, the Japanese quince, produces fruit which becomes useful for wildlife once it has dropped off and started to rot a little.

The last, and perhaps the most useful, range of garden flowers for the wildlife service station garden is the annuals. There is a massive selection of colourful plants which grow from seed to flowering age in a single season. Some of them should be started off in early spring and need the protection of a heated greenhouse or a warm windowsill at the seedling stage, but quite a number are perfectly hardy, and will fill your borders with colour for next to nothing. There are one or two biennials which are used as seasonal bedding, too.

The year begins with wallflowers, and certainly they get the pollen season off to a generous start. They are very easy to grow, so long as you remember to sow a year in advance, and the heady perfume in March is one of the real features of the spring garden. In milder gardens, wallflowers will live on for several years, but I've always found I need to plant fresh ones each autumn if I want a predictable display. Try to avoid planting wallflowers in the same spot year after year, they belong to the cabbage family and can suffer from clubroot.

Forget-me-nots are a great springtime favourite of mine. I love their powder blue colour, and if you give them a good shake as you pull up the spent plants you will produce a sheet of seedlings by late summer, ready for next year's display. Sweet williams come next, providing a very useful late spring nectar supply, and again surviving from year to year in milder districts, and there are polyanthus too, though you may be well advised to avoid these if you are trying to maintain a colony of native cowslips. The two are rather promiscuous, and you can end up with some very strangely-coloured cowslips in your meadow if they are close enough to interbreed.

Of the half-hardy summer garden flowers, I think nicotiana, the tobacco plant, is probably the most useful. There is a lime green variety, but most are mauve, pink or white, and they all have wonderful evening perfume. They can be planted out in late May, after the last frost, and will flower through until the autumn. I always grow tobacco flowers in pots by the front door, as well as in the main flower borders, and they reward me by bringing a whole variety of night-flying moths close to the house. I said earlier that single flowers tend to be better than doubles. This is true of the petunia, another half-hardy summer bedding plant worth growing for its pollen and nectar. The heliotrope, cherry pie, is a really good butterfly plant, and snapdragons are worth including, too. They have a very limited clientele, but make up for this by giving you lots of fun watching bumblebees struggling to force their way into each flower and then struggling to get out again.

The low, honey-perfumed bedding plant, white alyssum, is on the borderline between hardy and half-hardy. In the south it seeds on from year to year, in the same way as forget-me-nots, but further north you need to replant each spring. Plant a good big block of plants, at about 200mm centres, and by mid-summer you should have a continuous white carpet, and lots of nectar-sipping insects.

Half-hardy bedding tends to be rather expensive if you have to buy it. With all that winter heat it costs a lot to produce. If you are looking for cheaper alternatives, then there are plenty of very colourful hardy annuals available, and a packet of seed in April will give you masses of plants for next to nothing. There are lots of low-growing front-of-border species to choose from. Candytuft has flowers in the purple to white range, and seems popular with butterflies. Clarkia, virginia stock and larkspur are all in the same colour range and are better for bees. In the yellow and orange range you can produce spectacular results with a combination of hardy marigolds (*Calendula*) and Californian poppies. On sunny days, these flowers are alive with hoverflies of all shapes and sizes. All these low, annual flowering plants will flower on and on if you remove the dead heads as they fade. It is a natural survival strategy for plants to keep producing more and more flowers until they successfully set seed. This can be a pretty tedious job, particularly with flowers like the Californian poppies, where each bloom only lasts for a day, but it is well worth the effort. A couple of hardy annuals which produce seedlings

There are many useful 'hardy annuals' to grow. Sunflowers are particularly valuable because their nectar attracts both butterflies and bees, and dead seedheads provide food for tits and finches in autumn.

year after year, and spread around the garden, are Welsh poppy (*Mecanopsis cambrica*) and the poached egg plant (*Limnanthese douglassii*). The latter is particularly good for bees, hence its alternative name of bees' butter, and it is entirely covered with celandine-yellow flowers for the whole of June.

It is possible to achieve quite a lot of height with hardy annuals grown from seed. Cosmos has pink or purple flowers sprinkled over a thin structure of feathery-leaved stems, and will grow up to two metres tall. The prize for growth, though, must go to the sunflower, and you really should have a clump of these friendly giants in your wildlife service station. Seed planted in April will produce a plant as much as three metres tall by August, and the huge plates of florets glisten with nectar day after day. Both bees and butterflies feed on the 'faces', and in autumn you can expect a second performance when the more acrobatic of the garden birds move in and start stripping the seed. Greenfinches in particular are brilliant at tackling sunflower seed. They perch on top of the stem, seize the striped seed in their tough beak, spin it round like a can of beans, open up the outer skin and neatly remove the delicious kernel.

Old, dead stems may be a bit more untidy than you can cope with in your suburban garden, and if so, I suggest you cut the stems once the seed is ripe, and hang them upside down in a less prominent spot, where the birds can still get at them easily.

Finally, you might like to consider growing some of those colourful cornfield weeds as annual border flowers. Corncockle, for instance, is every bit as beautiful as the tobacco flowers, though it doesn't have their perfume. Our own native corn marigold is a very presentable alternative to accompany the Californian poppies in your yellow border, and of course our own scarlet poppies would be hard to beat for a real splash of colour. Cornflowers are always worth a place somewhere, and pheasant-eye looks far too exotic to be classified simply as a cornfield weed. There are vegetables which you can fit into your flower borders, too. I grow broad beans in mine, because I love the perfume, and the bees love the flowers. I grow courgettes because I've found nothing to beat the drama of their big floppy leaves, and their huge yellow flowers look very dramatic, and I usually have one or two of the poorer cabbage seedlings planted there, well away from the vegetable patch. The theory is that when the cabbages flower, they attract the cabbage white butterflies and they lay their eggs here, instead of fluttering off to infest the real crop. The problem is, no one seems to have told the butterflies.

Chapter 9

Fruit and veg and wildlife

THE HUMAN visitors to my wildlife garden always seem rather surprised to discover that I grow fruit and vegetables. They assume that would be out of the question with all this 'nature' around. In fact, the opposite is true. The pests that attack most gardeners' vegetables are actually kept under control pretty effectively by the predators from my rich habitats. Far from being a threat to the neighbours' gardens, I probably provide most of the ladybirds, hedgehogs and other pest-eaters that clean up their patches – unless, of course, they happen to be into wildlife gardening too, in which case they will have their own.

I must admit I am not a fanatical veg-grower. I simply don't have the time, but I do love to be able to pick a fresh lettuce or pull up a home-grown carrot in the summer, and despite the boom in pick-your-own soft fruit, I still think the raspberries picked and eaten straight from the garden do have a special flavour.

Apart from this 'freshness factor', the other important reason for growing your own is the reassurance it gives that for once you do know exactly what you are eating. The unblemished produce you buy in its poly-bags at the supermarket or pick for yourself in the countryside is only blemish-free because it is sprayed with pesticides as many as forty-six times in a season. Frankly, I heave a little sigh of relief if I find a caterpillar sharing my cauliflower. At least I know then that the veg can't be too heavily dosed. Given all the unsolicited extra ingredients we are forced to eat with even the freshest of food these days, there is something very reassuring about a plate of salad that I know has never been sprayed in its life. If the edges of the leaves look a little serrated, then I can smile to myself and know that I'm safe. The garden chemicals industry has done a magnificent job of building up their market. The garden centres are stacked out with bottles and packets of all kinds of poisons, presented as a means of giving you more wholesome fruit and vegetables. How crazy

Mixing flowers in your vegetable patch really does work. These marigolds attracted masses of predatory insects. Wasps, for instance, are a major wildlife garden predator and fly off to their nests with caterpillar after caterpillar. Many of the hoverflies have larvae which are predatory and very effective at wiping out aphids in particular.

can you get? Just look at a sepia photo of a farm labourer and his wife, standing proudly in their turn of the century cottage garden, surrounded by row upon row of prize cabbages, giant leeks and monster marrows. Chemicals have destroyed the balanced environment they enjoyed, and of course once you are hooked it's difficult to break the new artificial cycle. Once the first spray of the season wipes out your natural predators, you have to keep spraying the wave after wave of fast-recovery pests. Once you start using a root dip that protects against soil-borne infections, you no longer need to rotate the crops, and the pests are likely to build up to epidemic proportions that really would be devastating if you ever tried to kick the chemicals habit.

The alternative to all this dependence on poisonous chemicals is organic gardening. For years this has been seen as the domain of the 'nut-cutlet' brigade. Now, though, there is a green revolution going on all over Europe. Intelligent people are demanding far greater controls over commercial use of pesticides, and are 'growing their own' where they can. For the time being we may have to put up with chemical-rich bread, and according to research by Friends of the Earth, apparently as much as 64% of the pesticides sprayed on the farmers' wheat can still be there, unchanged, when you eat your sandwiches, but we don't have to live with the chemicals absorbed into potato skins, or broad beans, or broccoli – we can grow our own.

134

There are lots of publications dealing with organic gardening techniques. Much of the secret lies in sustaining high fertility by putting back plenty of organic compost as you crop, and of course the compost is only produced because there is a healthy workforce of fungi and micro-organisms available to convert the cabbage stems and lawn-clippings. For our purposes, though, I think it is most interesting to concentrate on the way the wildlife garden can positively help control pests and improve the quality of your produce.

The first suggestion is that you take a few simple precautions to protect your crops against the more obvious damage. You will attract a lot of birds with your wildlife service station gardening. Although you may know that your generosity ends at pyracantha berries and bruised windfalls, it is fair to assume that the blackbirds will try to extend the menu to raspberries, and the bullfinches will love the blackcurrant buds. A netted fruit cage is a simple, harmless way of defining the boundary between wildlife larder and human food-crop, and if you have serious problems with pigeons, for example, you can extend the idea to lower netted structures over your cabbages and Brussels sprouts.

There is also a range of intriguing devices for scaring away the larger forms of wildlife without harming them – persuading them to transfer their attention to the allotments down the road, in other words. Human look-alike scarecrows are not likely to be very effective. The local birds will already have marked you down as a soft touch and are not likely to be too worried by one of your old jumpers stuffed with straw. The fluttering and clattering kind of scarers are more effective, though I must say that in my garden the birds seem far too preoccupied with the natural food in the woodland-edge habitat or on the edge of the pond. They don't seem to show much interest in the relatively tidy veg-patch.

Small mammals can be a problem. Your log-pile might just house a rogue wood mouse that develops a taste for newly sown peas, though it hasn't happened to me yet. There are one or two folk remedies that are worth giving a whirl. How about inter-planting with the odd mothball, for instance, or perhaps you would prefer, as I do, to grow clumps of spearmint and the odd plant of caper spurge (*Euphorbia lactea*) amongst the vegetables. These two plants have a reputation for driving away both mice and moles, and since garden peas do end up sharing the saucepan with mint, it seems to make sense to have them living together first. There is actually a German battery-driven device on the market now which emits a piercing squeak at regular intervals. This is 'guaranteed' to frighten away any intruding mouse, but unless your vegetable patch is well away from the bedroom windows or you are exceptionally hard of hearing, I have a feeling you might crack rather sooner than the mice. Having mentioned the idea of growing mint and peas together, it is worth elaborating a little on the idea of companion planting. Years of accumulated knowledge have produced a whole host of suggestions for crop-plants which seem in some mysterious way to protect and promote one another, and also a number of partnerships which are counter-productive. If you are interested, I suggest you get a book on the subject out of the library, but one particular idea is well worth discussing in detail. There is undoubtedly a great advantage to be gained by growing flowers amongst your vegetables, and by having a patch or two of 'weeds' close by too. Most people will probably smile at that suggestion, having dreamed for years of the day when there is *not* a mass of weeds in the vegetable patch. What I am suggesting is that they should be positively encouraged – within reason, of course.

There are two reasons for growing flowers. Some of them do seem to have a chemical influence on the soil, and help control or at least suppress some of the pests and diseases. All of them attract pollinating insects, and many of these are of great benefit in the vegetable patch. Marigolds are the most celebrated of all 'companion flowers', and I have grown them amongst my carrots, beans and broccoli for years. The hardy annual *Calendula officinalis* apparently has a devastating effect on eel worms – a serious group of soil-borne pests which can destroy onions, potatoes and several other crops. Rotating the crops helps stop the pests building up in numbers, but marigolds actually seem to kill them off. In fact, commercial organic growers sow a green-manure crop of marigold every few years, to clean up their soil before replanting with vegetables. I also grow French and African marigolds in blocks each year. They actually do smell as if they ought to be doing some good. The leaves are quite pungent, and perhaps that is a clue to this aspect of their mysterious success as pest-repellants.

Marigolds are also very good in the vegetable patch, because they are particularly popular with hoverflies and wasps. Although the adults feed on pollen, and the common wasp will gorge itself on rotten fruit too, they are also very important predators. Between them they provide an amazingly efficient control against cabbage-white caterpillars, and they will devastate many other grubs, larvae and aphids, given half a chance. The various types of wasps and hoverflies operate in quite different ways. The common wasp collects caterpillars from the vegetable patch, and everywhere else in your garden, and flies off with them to the nest. Here the prey is stored in a larder, and when the wasp eggs themselves hatch, the grubs feed on the accumulated food store. Just stand and watch your cabbage patch for a few minutes in the height of summer; you are sure to see wasp after wasp patrolling over the leaves, and then suddenly dropping like a stone on to some poor, unsuspecting pest, and buzzing off back to base with their juicy cargo hanging helplessly from their undercarriage. Many of the garden hoverflies produce predatory larvae which kill aphids and other pests, and the ichneumons and brachonids lay their eggs inside living caterpillars on your cabbages. The pest continues to munch away for a little while longer, but when the larvae themselves hatch, they eat away the host caterpillar from the inside. It's not a pretty thought, I know, but these natural predators and parasites really are very efficient if you give them half a chance.

The weed patch works in a similar though less clearly understood way. Few if any of the weed species are likely to harbour pests and diseases that attack crop plants, but they may well harbour preferred prey species which attract more predators. These are then likely to move across on to the crop pests. Whatever the reason, if you can grow a patch or two of weeds, kept separate so that they don't compete with the veg for moisture or food, that does seem to help reduce the problem of vegetable garden pests and diseases.

Slugs and snails can be a bit of a menace, particularly to young seedlings in wet weather. A path of coarse bark around the veg-patch seems to put a lot of them off, and certainly the vast majority of the many slugs and snails in my own garden never go anywhere near the vegetables. They are far too contented browsing on the fallen leaves and fungi of the woodland edge and the hedge bottom. I do have some very efficient slug-gobblers helping me, too. The toads eat a great many. A few minutes standing in the dark listening to the hedgehogs chomping and snuffling through the undergrowth will confirm that an enormous number meet a sticky end that way, and on one or two sacrificial stones around the garden there are piles of broken snail shells, left behind as evidence of the songthrush's favourite pastime – snail-bashing.

If you can't wait for nature to sort out the slugs, then please don't resort to poisons. The slug pellets may be labelled as 'harmless to hedgehogs', but when the hedgehogs eat the poisoned slugs, that is a different story. One hedgehog can get through dozens of slugs and snails in a night, and the poison quickly builds up to a deadly concentration. There are ways of trapping or killing slugs which have far less environmental risk attached. I know quite a few people who put down half-grapefruit skins around the edge of their vegetable crops. The slugs gather underneath them, and are then escorted carefully to some distant wilderness. It is no good just tossing them over the fence into next door's garden, however tempting that may be, because these amazing creatures have a very effective homing facility, and will simply slide back under the fence when you turn your back.

If you must kill them, slugs are easy to tempt into a sump filled with beer. You can buy fancy plastic devices with roofs on to stop hedgehogs and other slug gourmets getting at the corpses, but a plastic cup sunk into the ground, and protected with a couple of stones will suffice just as well. The sweet, sticky liquid seems to be preferable to even the most juicy of lettuces, and once the slugs fall in, they can't climb out. If the hedgehog

Let nature protect your crops. Ladybirds and their larvae are extremely efficient at catching blackfly. If you spray your broadbeans you will almost certainly kill the ladybirds, and they take far longer to 'bounce back' than the pests do.

does manage to pick up a stomach full of beer-soaked slugs then the worst after-effect it can expect is a hangover. Presumably, when this happens he will be even pricklier than usual the following morning!

There is one final tactic which helps me to grow perfectly respectable fruit and vegetables without needing to spray. I avoid species which are particularly difficult. I generally grow a copper-leaved variety of lettuce, for instance, because the birds simply don't seem tempted by it at all. I grow climbing French beans but generally avoid the dwarf forms. All those little tender beans dangling at ground level are too tempting for the slugs, but when suspended several feet in the air they seem relatively safe. I grow broad beans every year, and pinch out the tops at the first sign of blackfly. I grow wonderful carrots, but sow thinly enough never to need to thin at the seedling stage, and this seems to help them escape attack from carrot-root fly. That particular pest is also put off by a nearby crop of leeks. I grow courgettes and tomatoes in pots out of slugs' reach until they are big enough and tough enough to survive the odd bit of casual chewing. I grow winter broccoli because it crops when very few pests are around, and I grow lots of rhubarb, Jerusalem artichokes and ruby chard because *nothing* seems to like eating their leaves. My sandy soil produces very clean potatoes unaided, though I appreciate that little black keel slugs can be a problem on wet ground. If I plant broad beans amongst the spuds they both seem to benefit.

By creating a garden for wildlife you are giving yourself a real advantage in the vegetable-growing stakes. It seems a shame not to make the most of it. Your encouragement of predators like ladybirds, toads and robins provides you with a resident pesticide squad, and if you choose what you grow wisely, protect against crop damage where practical, and put up with the odd happy little poison-free caterpillar in your salad from time to time, then there is no reason why you and your garden wildlife can't walk off with the prizes at the local show.

Chapter 10

Artificial habitat boosters

THE COMMONEST positive garden wildlife conservation gesture most people make is to put up a birdtable. In fact there is a whole host of ways in which your wildlife service station can be made more attractive to the passing trade. The boost to plant life, to pollen and seed supply, has already been discussed. Now it is time to think about other ways of creating a super-habitat.

A birdtable is a good idea. It gives you an opportunity to attract a wide range of wild creatures to a spot where you can watch them and enjoy their company in comfort. The table itself doesn't need to be sophisticated at all. What really matters is the way you use it. You must take the responsibility seriously. Once you begin putting out a supply of food, the birds from quite a wide area will quickly come to rely on you, and they can suffer badly if the free handouts suddenly stop appearing. It is a good idea to feed at regular times each day. For me, that tends to be just after breakfast. It is convenient as a way of using up the toast crumbs, and in the depths of winter it means the food is there as it gets light, and the birds emerge from another cold night, desperate for life-giving food. Although I am away from the house most days during the week, this early morning ritual has the added advantage that when I am at home, at the weekend for example, I can enjoy the squabbles that follow through the rest of the day.

The siting of the birdtable really is critical. In fact you should be thinking of a 'feeding station' rather than limiting yourself to a table alone. Quite a few garden birds are very reluctant to feed four or five feet above the ground, and prefer to peck and scratch around at ground level. Hedge sparrows and wrens feed here, for example, and so some open ground around the base of the table is useful if you want to watch.

The principal advantage of a feeding station is that it helps you study the birds. The first consideration, therefore, should be your convenience.

Choose a spot which will give you unrestricted viewing from one or more of your busy windows. My birdtable is about four feet from the kitchen window, and provides some encouragement to do the washing up. It is also important to have a nice, convenient route from the house to the birds. A fifty yard trek down the garden with the birdseed may be fine on a sunny day in November, but when the snow is four feet thick, you will be grateful for a nice short, paved route, and that will help to encourage you to keep up the regular service when it is most needed.

If you concentrate your wildlife anywhere, the word will quickly get round to the local predators. In August I am 'entertained', if that is the right word, by spotted fly-catchers gathering on the trees around the buddleia bush, and swooping down to snatch the tipsy small tortoise-shells delicately in mid-flight. The cabbages on the vegetable patch become a focus for the wasps' attention once they start to generate a steady production line of caterpillars, and night after night the bats visit my pond – grateful, no doubt, for the concentration of aquatic insect life I have so graciously provided for them. The birdtable falls into the same category. It gathers together a regular, noisy concentration of birds and that is bound to arouse the interest of predators. Top of the pecking order in most neighbourhoods is the local domestic cat. You may have the odd sparrowhawk playing out its textbook sparrow-snatching role occasionally, but cats are the real menace, and you must take the problem seriously when you take on a birdtable. Don't put it too close to potential moggie-cover. Bushes and small trees are fine, so long as they are more than a leap away – perhaps two metres as a minimum. In fact the birds will appreciate a handy branch to fly up to at any sign of danger. I actually have a substantial twig fixed into a hole in my birdtable, and it is surprising how many birds perch there first, before actually daring to land on the table.

If cats are a serious threat to your bird-watching, then there are a number of things you can do to help. Keeping a dog, or even better a rather overweight and dopey neutered tom cat yourself is supposed to be the ultimate deterrent, though I must confess I find the prospect of this cure rather unattractive. A large bell around the neck of each of the offending local cats will at least give the birds a bit of warning. An inverted metal cone around the leg of the birdtable will make it difficult for the cats to climb up, and a table which is five feet tall, rather than the usual four feet, should put it beyond the reach of all but the most athletic of leaping pussies. If none of these precautions work, try hanging the table (or the cat) from a branch. It will swing there freely and be far too unstable to carry the cat.

Another possible hazard you introduce by bringing together a high concentration of birds is the risk of promoting infectious diseases. For this reason, it is advisable to move the station each year, though in a small garden that might be rather difficult. You should also make sure you don't overfeed and allow food to lie uneaten. If there is an accumulation of stale food, that too can cause health problems for the birds, and it is quite likely to attract scavengers such as rats, too. I suspect that this is not the kind of garden wildlife most people are keen to be watching from the kitchen window.

The choice of food you offer will affect the range of birds you see. You need to provide both hard and soft foods. The housesparrows, tits and finches have tough beaks and are happy cracking sunflower seeds and corn, but the insect-eaters with the pointed bills are not likely to feed unless you provide lumps of fat for them. Bread is not a very healthy diet

OPPOSITE: In winter the main feature of the service station wildlife garden will be your bird feeding station. Different species have different feeding habits and you must provide a regular supply of a variety of foods. Great-tits and bluetits feed on fat and monkeynuts hanging from the birdtables. Siskins, greenfinches and even woodpeckers have learned to attack peanuts in orange nylon bags. Starlings will peck away at marrow bones and robins love little pieces of cheese. Include a range of seeds for the sparrows and finches and make sure you put apples and other food on the ground for the blackbirds, thrushes, fieldfares and redwings. Make sure your birdtable is beyond the reach of the most agile pussycat.

for birds, although they do get through tons of the stuff each winter.

One or two species are especially fond of a particular type of food. Greenfinches will always go for the sunflower seed first. Coaltits will carry away peanut after peanut to their private larder, but will leave all the other seeds untouched. Siskins seem to have developed a taste for peanuts in plastic nets in recent years; robins are passionate about mature cheddar; blackbirds, fieldfares and redwings are at their most contented pecking away at soft over-ripe apples on the lawn. I pester my local fruit shop for bruised fruit from November onwards and it really does bring in the birds.

We had a songthrush at one time that was really fond of cherries. It would collect them from the back doorstep, flutter off to a safe spot a few feet away, and then roll the fruit around in the dust with its beak, with exactly the same sideways action it used for slugs. When the cherry was suitably scruffy it would swallow it whole, and hop back for a second helping.

If you live in an area with woodland or large, old hedgerow trees nearby, you may be lucky enough to have woodpeckers visiting you. They do come down to the orange nets of peanuts, and once they learn the trick they waste no time in ripping open the net. None of that earnest, onerous chipping away that the naive little bluetits go in for. You can save on plastic nets, and possibly increase your chances of a longer woodpecker-visit, by making a 'suet log'. Both the greater and lesser spotted woodpeckers find a great deal of their natural food by working away with their sharp beaks behind the bark of old silver birch trees. If you can get your hands on a couple of feet of birch log – preferably dead and going rotten – then you can provide a very tempting lure quite easily. Just gouge out a hole or two from the log and fill these with a mixture of soft fat and bird seed. Then hang the log vertically so it swings from a convenient branch. If there is a woodpecker anywhere in the neighbourhood, you are most likely to persuade it to become a regular garden visitor.

This fascination woodpeckers have for dead birch logs can be a mixed blessing. A friend of mine made the mistake of using silver birch for the leg of his birdtable. He was thrilled when the local woodpecker began visiting the table regularly, but not quite so enchanted when it hopped underneath and pecked the post to bits.

One of the nice things about all the correspondence I receive, is the discovery that bird populations develop local specialities. Presumably the first great-tit to discover the delights that lay beneath the milkbottle top was a 'hyperactive, gifted fledgling'. The trick was obviously spotted by the local competition, and caught on with a vengeance. Both greenfinches and siskins have learned the peanut-bag trick only very recently, and in at least one garden I know there are now starlings that

Many garden birds migrate to Britain for the winter. These siskins are benefiting from a bag of peanuts, but their favourite food is alder seed.

can manage this feat. I don't imagine they look quite so much at home hanging upside down as the bluetits do, though.

Nestboxes are the other established technique for habitat boosting. In fact in most urban areas there would be very few bluetits and great-tits around to bother with your peanuts if it wasn't for the artificial nesting sites people provide. Many of our popular garden birds would naturally nest inside hollow tree trunks, or the cavities in rotten branches; tiny little things like the bluetit, and relative giants like the tawny owl. Our tidymindedness and our preoccupation with public safety have made sure that there are very, very few dead trees, or even dead branches, permitted in town, and so many of these adopted woodland birds have had to adapt a little. Most species of bats use the same sort of tree sites to roost, breed and hibernate too, and their numbers have plummeted alarmingly as we have made more and more of them homeless. Batboxes are more urgently needed than birdboxes these days, since at least two species of these incredible little flying mammals are faced with imminent extinction, and most of the rest of the species have been reduced in numbers by a third to a half in ten years.

There is a lot more to nestboxes than you might think. The actual design of the box greatly influences the choice of resident you are likely to attract, and positioning is all important too. The simplest boxes to build

Nestboxes are safer on walls than in trees, and do make sure they are never positioned where they can get baked by the direct sun.

143

are little more than a flat, open tray – just an artificial ledge for the bird to build on. A piece of wood 100 to 150mm square, with a 30mm upstand around the edge, is all you need. Fix this little tray a couple of metres high on to a wall where it will be camouflaged by the leaves of climbers, and you could well attract nesting spotted flycatchers. These pretty little migrant birds don't arrive here from Africa until May, but if you do get adopted by a pair, then they and their descendants are likely to visit you year after year. If you put the tray a little lower, you may attract nesting robins, and if there is a lot of cover, blackbirds and songthrushes will use it. This is a good habitat booster to fix in the space you have provided beyond the curtain of climbers on your garden fence or wall.

The same platform design can be used to accommodate swallows. These superbly streamlined summer visitors nest inside buildings. In the countryside they fly in and out through an open barn door, and often build their modest little mud nest on a rafter or a beam. They are still not all that common in towns, but you may just persuade a pair to join you for the summer if you leave the door of the garden shed or the outside lav permanently ajar, and fix the tray up high in a corner, where the swallows have a clear flight path in and out. If the swallows don't find it then robins, wrens and blackbirds are all possible takers.

Most of the tray-nesting birds will also build in open-fronted boxes. These are really little more than a basic tray with three sides and a roof, and they are generally sold by the RSPB and others under the name of robin-boxes. They don't need quite so much camouflage as the open tray, but they too are far better placed on a wall than a tree. A whole range of egg and chick thieves are able to climb or land in trees, and the open-fronted box is very vulnerable. On a wall the only predator that is still a serious threat is the magpie. Give your box a good overhang and make sure there isn't a handy perch within reach, otherwise the magpies will have the whole nest out in no time.

If you have the right site available, you might like to put up a bigger version of the robin-box. Make the nest tray about 400mm square, and allow for about 300mm of headroom. If you put the box high up inside an empty building – say an old Victorian coach house or a warehouse – and position it close to an opening in the wall, you may be lucky enough to attract barn owls. These are the wonderful creamy white hunters that you very occasionally spot flapping like giant moths across a country lane in front of your headlights. Old barns have been replaced by modern weatherproof (and owl-proof) asbestos hangers these days, and the barn owl needs all the help we can provide. If you fix your big box to the outside of the building, rather than the inside, there are a couple of species of bird that may use it. Put it very high up – even the top of a twenty-storey tower block isn't too far from the ground – and you are quite likely to pull in a pair of kestrels. These magnificent predators have become very familar since they have staked out their territory along the rough verges of the motorways. They can be seen hanging menacingly over the small mammal habitat of urban wasteland, too, living up to their lovely old name of wind-hover, and most of the urban birds nest high on buildings. A nestbox provides them with the perfect weatherproof shady ledge. Town pigeons will welcome a big box too, if it is a little lower down.

The most familiar nestbox is the one that looks like a closed box with a small hole in it. The best material is probably unstained, rough cut timber, though you can now buy pre-moulded plastic boxes (which may tend to sweat); there are waxed-paper boxes, terracotta pot ones, and all sorts of weird and wonderfully decorated mini-thatched cottages and half-timbered black and white mock-Tudor boxes. The more subdued they are, the better. The name of the game is camouflage, not neon-lit advertisement.

The size of the hole has a great influence on who moves in. Basically, the bigger it is, the greater will be the range of species that can squeeze in, and what tends to happen is that the biggest bird wins. A tiny hole just 30mm in diameter will leave bluetits with sole possession. Go up 5mm in size and great-tits can manage to squeeze through, and the bluetits lose control. A 50mm hole opens up the market to sparrows and robins, and if you go any bigger, you are most likely to finish up housing starlings year after year.

Woodpeckers do occasionally nest in large 'tit' boxes, and obviously they are well equipped to hack away until the hole is whatever size they need. They usually reserve this particular performance until the box is already occupied, however, and enlarge the hole with the much more sinister intention of gobbling up the eggs or baby birds. If you have the rather colourful problem of robber woodpeckers in your garden, you can thwart a lot of them by reinforcing the hole with a punched-out metal plate, but despite all that head-banging, woodpeckers are very far from stupid, and it won't take them long to work out that they can chop out a perfectly adequate hole of their own through the unprotected wood in the other side of the box.

Most box-nesting birds will adjust the entrance hole a little when they decide to move in. This seems to be a part of their territorial marking procedure. There was a great-tit in the garden one year that tapped and pecked away all round the hole for days and days, despite the fact that he could squeeze in and out without any difficulty. Nuthatches actually prefer a hole which starts off being too large, and they reverse the chipping process by narrowing down the opening with a ring of mud until it is just the right size for them. Tree creepers only seem happy nesting in a special wedge-shaped box that presumably feels like their natural nesting site, the gap behind a loose piece of peeling bark, and tawny owls will nest in another, much bigger type of box which is known as an owl 'chimney'. This is a long, square 'tube' of wood, open at the top end and with drainage holes at the bottom. It needs to have internal dimensions of about 200 by 200mm, and be at least 600mm long. If you fix it very securely on top of a sturdy branch, preferably at a slight angle and at least ten metres above the ground, you may have the great privilege of being kept awake night after night by lovesick screech owls practising their horror-movie sound effects outside your bedroom window.

Swifts give me more pleasure than any other bird I know. They seem to symbolise everything that is wild and free, and they really have a quite incredible lifestyle. There is a considerable colony in my neighbourhood, perhaps fifty or sixty pairs breeding each summer in this one suburban street. They are one of the wild species that has adopted high manmade buildings as their primary nesting habitat, but our Edwardian house is too well built, and they can't seem to find any gaps which give them access to the roofspace. Of all the houses in the street, this is the only one that has neither swifts nor their fellow travellers, the housemartins, nesting on or in it. I have done something about that now, though. Both these species will happily nest in boxes, provided they are specially built for them. The swifts need something rather similar to an owl chimney on its side, with both ends blocked off and a narrow, 25mm slot under the front end for the birds to fly up and into. I am fixing these under the eaves of the house in the hope that one day they might be occupied. At the beginning of August every year the young, newly-fledged swifts flutter all around the house, presumably searching under the eaves for holes which they can return to for egg-laying a couple of years later, so with any luck my strange-looking boxes will be imprinted on some globe-trotting swift or two by now.

Housemartins have quite a different approach to nesting. They build their own solid little mud-hut, glued tightly to the underside of a windowsill or a roof overhang. They seem to build mostly on new houses, and one reason must be the plentiful supply of wet mud to be found on building sites. I get housemartins collecting mud from the edge of the pond, but they fly straight past my desirable and eager residence, and insist on building in full view of my desk, beside the bay window of the post-war semi across the road.

I have put up a number of off-the-peg pre-cast concrete martinboxes. They look very convincing to me, and since housemartins seem to like building little colonies of mud nests I hoped that, even if they didn't actually occupy the nestboxes, they might build one or two of their own on the same wall – but so far nothing has happened. I read somewhere that damage to last year's nest is thought to trigger off the returning birds' nest-building instinct, so I have snapped a few lumps off my

concrete in the hope that the birds might have read the same article, but I have a funny suspicion that they just watch my desperate measures with mild, muddy amusement.

The really frustrating thing is that the chap down the road, whose house is a veritable holiday-camp for housemartins, can't stand the mess they make – and keeps knocking the nests off with a stick.

I said that swifts were my most inspiring birds. It is partly their wild disregard for all of us that I admire. I share the thrill they seem to be enjoying as they scream in high-speed squadrons over the garden, and I envy their tremendous command of the air. It is the story of their lifecycle that really captivates me, though. When the two eggs hatch, the parents feed the young with thousands of insects and spiders caught on the wing.

Dry stone walls make marvellous habitats for both plants and animals to colonise. Here herb robert (*Geranium robertianum*) has taken up residence.

Eventually the fledglings venture to the mouth of the nest-hole, and with all the courage of a first-time parachutist, they just launch themselves into the air. There is no time for practising. You either fly or you have had it, and amazingly that young bird will not land again for two years. The only time swifts land is when they have eggs to lay and young to feed, and it takes two years to reach maturity. In that time the young birds will fly over half a million miles, nipping over to Hungary or up to Denmark for a couple of days of rich feeding if the insects are a bit sparse at home, and climbing thousands of metres up into the sky each evening, to glide effortlessly on the wing, and sleep through the hours of darkness. Swifts are migratory birds. They spend the winter amongst the clouds of insects in the warmth of Africa, and return to northern Europe each summer to breed. The round trip is about 8000 miles, and the most incredible thing of all is that each year the newly-fledged young birds leave a couple of weeks ahead of their parents. They find their own way south of the Sahara or beyond the Nile, with no help from mum, and they then find their own way back to our street the following May. The idea that by spending half an hour one winter's evening knocking up a nestbox, I might be privileged enough to play a small part in that miracle is one of the things that makes attracting wildlife really exciting for me. Even if I don't actually succeed in providing nesting accommodation, I get a great kick out of sharing the midges from my pond and the butterflies from the meadow with long-distance travellers like the swift, the swallow, the housemartin, the chiffchaff and the flycatcher.

Birds aren't the only wild creatures you can persuade to move into artificial homes. You can set up tempting potential residence for a whole host of animals, from large mammals such as the fox and the hedgehog down to tiny creatures like solitary bees and hunting spiders. The secret is to use your imagination. Try and think of yourself as an earwig looking for somewhere to hibernate, or a queen bee on the hunt for a suitable new nest-site. Think yourself into the role of a pregnant vixen looking for just the right secluded spot in which to have her litter of cubs. If you can think this way as you build up your wildlife garden, you will find yourself incorporating all kinds of extra little 'wildlife opportunities' – little wrinkles in the landscape which you think might appeal to some homeless plant or animal.

Urban foxes are well known for living under garden sheds. They need a nice dry, shallow hole which is safe, and which ideally offers at least two exits. If you are putting in a new shed, you have a choice to make. Do you put it on a floor of solid concrete, and rule out any chance of housing foxes, or do you opt for a shed with a timber floor, and set it on foundations of railway sleepers or concrete footings, allowing for a gap beneath the shed which might become adopted?

There are some quite fanciful designs around for 'hedgehog houses'.

They are fun to play about with if you have time on your hands, but you can create a pretty useful hibernating site much more simply by piling three or four substantial logs together so that they create a hedgehog-sized hole, and then covering the whole structure with masses of leaves and dead twigs.

One very useful way of concentrating a variety of mini-homes or niches together in one spot is to build a dry-stone and earth bank. Stack stones randomly to form a double-sided wall, with a space in the centre. Keep incorporating layers of soil and fill the centre too. Make sure you leave lots of little holes through the stone facing which lead to bigger gaps in the centre. A whole range of very pretty wildflowers like wall habitats. Herb robert is a favourite of mine – a small member of the cranesbill family with a cut leaf and red stems. Stone crop (*Sedum acre*) will quickly spread along the earth joints, and cover the stone bank with its little yellow star-shaped flowers in summer. Harebells (*Campanula rotundifolia*), ivy-leaved toadflax and primroses will thrive, and if it is fairly shady and not too dry, a whole range of lovely native ferns can be persuaded to become established, too.

You will quickly find the creepy-crawly end of the animal world moving into your bank. There are lots of nooks and crannies to hide in, and hunting spiders, woodlice and ants will be there in no time. If you pack one or two of the inner cavities with old nesting material from a mouse-cage, you will be providing irresistible conditions for queen bumblebees to occupy, and you can create several bee-nest sites elsewhere in the garden, by burying clay plant pots in banks and shrub-beds, so that just the hole in the bottom is visible. If more mouse-bedding is stuffed inside these pots, you will have bees flying busily in and out of the drainage hole by mid-summer.

Quite a lot of insects lay their eggs in tiny, narrow holes. Remember the woodwasps of the woodland-edge log-piles do that. Quite a few beetles are wood-boring by nature, and solitary bees are fascinating little creatures that will occupy other insects' vacated holes. You can simulate this tiny niche by drilling lots of holes in the logs yourself, or in your fenceposts, perhaps. Some of the species will also oblige by occupying the holes created when you tie a bundle of drinking straws together and block up one end. Hang your little bundles under ledges and overhangs and wait for the insects to investigate.

If you look closely at old brickwork, you will discover that it is extensively colonised by all kinds of things. New brickwork takes a very long time to acquire its 'hangers-on', but you can speed up the process quite easily. Take a masonry drill and bore a few holes in the mortar. In no time you will find the entrance to these manmade tunnels decorated by a swirl of gossamer, and a light brush, preferably with a tuning fork or a feather, will bring the resident spider rushing out. Old walls support lots of the lower forms of plant life too, such as algae and liverworts, and in the relatively unpolluted atmosphere of modern towns and cities, we are again beginning to see lots of lichens. You can have quite an impact on the rate of colonisation if you paint a coat of 'magic mixture' on the surface of the brick. My particular brew is made of a very thin flour and milk paste, souped up with just a dash of cow slurry or bottled liquid manure. Initially you will probably be rewarded with nothing more interesting than a crop of dull mould, but within a month or two you will begin to see the surface patterns change, and if you compare treated and untreated walls you will realise how much effect you have had.

There really is no end to the ways you can enhance the garden habitats. A sheet of old corrugated iron laid out in the meadow will heat up in the sun and could well accommodate slow-worms as well as the more predictable centipedes and beetles. A chunk of paving slab in the woodland edge will often be used by ants as a lid to their underground nest. I used a spare corner of butyl pondliner to create a tiny little artificial puddle amongst the logs. This is now completely overgrown with deadnettle and grasses, but amazingly enough each generation of tiny little frogs that emerges from the main pond seems to head instinctively for the little bit of shady dampness, crossing lawn and meadow to get there. I have counted as many as forty of these perfect miniatures in an area not much larger than a couple of dinner plates.

Some friends have a very small walled yard, with nowhere in which to create a leaflitter habitat, or anything resembling a woodland-edge. They had the bright idea of fixing a panel of several different planks of wood to form a kind of sculpture just an inch or so proud of the wall. Visitors admire this piece of 'modern art' but the real magic of their creation is the colony of bats that roost behind the boarding, and the range of wasps and other wood-boring creatures that are gradually perforating the timber.

Do be inventive. Do think about the way wildlife will use your garden, and if you see some creature making unorthodox use of one of your artificial aids, so much the better. A good many bird nestboxes are used by hibernating moths, butterflies and bats in the winter. The hole I left in the brickwork of my patio wall, as a 'perfect nesting-site for wrens' has been occupied each year by bees. The bark chippings I put down to suppress the weed problem have proved tremendously successful as a hunting-ground for the perfectly camouflaged hunting spiders. Even the half-brick-sized gap I cursed the builder for leaving under the eaves of the extension has been put to good use. For two years in a row the little cock wren has built there. The first year his mate turned down the accommodation in favour of one of the alternatives he had on offer. The second year, though, she graciously moved in and succeeded in raising a fine brood of six beautiful babies.

There is one final habitat-booster that should find a place in everybody's garden. That is the compost heap. We all produce mountains of waste greenery every year. Cabbage leaves, potato peel, weed seedlings, the excess waterweed from the pond; they all make wonderful compost if you allow time for them to rot down, and it is so much better than burning and binning them. The ideal spot for a compost heap is in a shady corner, out of sight of the house, but reasonably convenient for deliveries of kitchen waste. You need some sort of perforated container – either well-spaced timber planking, or well-staked netting, and the bottom of the heap should rest on the soil. You must make sure plenty of air is able to circulate around the heap, and you may need to protect it against heavy rain with a tarpaulin or a sheet of polythene if the heap is out in the open. The softer material rots down fastest. Twiggy material – hedge clippings and rose prunings, for example – is better stacked separately or used to make hibernation habitat. A heap built up through the summer should be turned into sweet-smelling crumbly compost and ready to use the following spring.

The whole business of compost-making relies entirely on the vigorous activity of plant and animal life, and that is what makes a compost heap such a marvellous asset in the wildlife garden. Most of the actual organisms of decay are minute – far too small for you to see with the naked eye – but you can tell they are at work by the way they generate heat, and on a chilly morning you should see wisps of steam rising from a well-constructed compost heap. There are larger decomposers too. If you pull back the top layer of your heap you will find a network of white filaments of fungal mycelia, and you will also see a whole host of different creepy-crawlies. Some of them, most noticeably the bright red little worms, are living directly on the dead plant material, and breaking it down to a size that the smaller micro-organisms can cope with, but there will be lots of predators in your compost heap, too. There will be beetles and centipedes, and a number of other fast-moving wriggly creatures, eating up the smaller organisms of decay, and feeding on any bits of animal remains that you add to the heap. With so much going on, it is not surprising to find that the compost heap becomes an important 'fast food section' of your service station wildlife garden. Some of the bigger creatures may spend almost the whole time there. You are quite likely to have a fat, contented toad or two living in the moist warmth of the heap, gorging themselves on some of the hardworking slugs, and your resident hedgehog may move into the compost corner too, at least for the summer, starting each evening's ramble with a tasty compost-grown snack before moving off around the rest of the garden.

The heat generated by the compost heap is an important feature of the habitat. It speeds up the rate of decomposition, but it also provides ideal conditions for one or two of our more delicate wild animals to breed in. Slow-worms in particular like to give birth to their tiny babies in the warmth of a compost heap, and grass-snakes very often lay their eggs there. Both of these creatures are perfectly harmless, and marvellous additions to your wildlife garden. The grass-snakes may get through quite a few of your frogs and toads, and being spectacular swimmers they can also catch small fish occasionally, but the slow-worm has a diet made up mainly of slugs and worms, and really does nothing but good. Both of these creatures are persecuted in the wild, largely by people who simply think all 'snakes' are deadly poisonous. If you build a compost heap, put in a pond, leave some of the lawn a little longer and stack the odd log-pile around in your shrubbery, you will be providing the ideal habitat for slow-worms and grass-snakes to visit and to stay, and your garden will become a safe sanctuary for two increasingly rare and very handsome wild creatures.

Chapter 11

Propagating native plants

NATIVE PLANTS are the basic ingredient which turns your garden into a rich habitat for wildlife. The choice of species is enormous. Hundreds of different types of wildflowers, shrubs and trees grow wild in our countryside. Some of them are very common, and some are extremely rare. Very few of them are available 'off the shelf'' in garden centres. If you want a garden full of wildflowers, then you are going to have to 'do it yourself'. Do ask your local garden centre first, though. Native plants are gradually creeping into the market place, and the more requests a garden centre manager receives, the more likely he is to begin stocking the wildlife plants you need.

You stand a reasonable chance of buying native trees and shrubs without too much trouble. Species like hazel, silver birch and beech have been grown commercially for years. Even the less 'gardeny' native shrubs such as field maple, wild rose and goat willow, whilst they may not actually be stocked by the garden centre, are grown on a vast scale for planting on motorway embankments, countryside projects and in the more enlightened of local authority parks. If you pester them, your garden centre should be able to get them for you.

Very often you will find that these 'native' trees and shrubs are in fact imported, and therefore not really ideal for habitat creation. Sometimes a wholesale nurseryman will buy in the plants himself, from Holland or Germany in particular. Even when the plants are actually home-grown, the nurseryman very often uses imported seed, so your 'English alder', your elderberry or your silver birch could well be a European subspecies and may lead to rather disappointing results. Do ask your nurseryman if he is selling British-grown plants from indigenous seed-stock. The odds are he may not even understand the question, but if enough people ask, and then explain the significance of native plants for nature conservation, eventually the nursery industry will get the message.

Road-side verges are becoming increasingly important for wildlife. Here a patch of wildflowers is benefiting from the low cost management and will provide a useful source of seed in late summer.

There are a growing number of nurseries around which specialise in native wildflowers. They are mostly fairly small, but as the demand grows, they will no doubt increase production. One or two of them are extremely good. I buy most of my pot-grown wildflowers from a specialist nurseryman in Somerset, and his list now contains virtually every wildflower you could wish to grow in your garden. I bought some superb plants of devil's bit scabious from him last year, to provide food for the caterpillars of some marsh-fritillary butterflies, and the five plants filled a square metre of my garden with a wonderful display of blue flowers throughout August and September.

The seed of wildflowers is increasingly easy to come by, but again foreign stock is widespread. This can be quite a serious problem, as the foreign strain of some of our wildflowers is much more vigorous than the native type, and if we start sprinkling the super-seedlings around our towns and villages, some of the plants are certain to escape, and could well overwhelm the indigenous stock. The more responsible seedhouses are very particular about this point. They go to great pains to obtain seed from truly native wildflowers wherever they can, and if it proves impossible and they have to resort to a foreign seed source, then they make this quite clear, both in their catalogues and on the packets. There is not much risk in a town garden in the heart of the city, but if your

wildlife garden is in a rural village, or even the leafy suburbs, do try and restrict your seed purchases exclusively to native stock. Most of the specialist nurseries will ship plants through the post, so it is worth sending off an S.A.E. for the catalogues. There is a short list of recommended seed suppliers and specialist wildflower nurseries at the back of the book.

Of course, packets of seed and nursery-grown potted plants are the easy way – but however conscientious your suppliers are, the very best way to stock your wildlife garden is by growing your own plants, using the seed of wild plants which are not just native to Britain, but actually native to your own local landscape. These are truly indigenous plants, and they will be very intimately locked into the local climate, soil-type and the indigenous wildlife, too. Local wildflowers, trees and shrubs should be the source of your wildlife garden plants – *but!!* you must *never* dig up any wild plant and move it to your garden – however common it might seem to be. Wild plants are protected by the law, and that law is there for a very good reason. Digging up wild plants will eventually lead to their disappearance in the wild. As a wildlife gardener your aim should be to provide an *extra* habitat, not simply to rob one in order to create another.

Fortunately, it is quite easy to grow new plants without harming the

Old graveyards are often sanctuaries for wildlife. This churchyard has obviously escaped the pressure of modern chemicals and its wildflowers can provide a useful source for the wildlife gardener.

parent plant growing in the wild. The simple secret is to collect seed, or in a few cases to take a cutting or two. For a number of especially rare wildflowers it is illegal to remove any part of these plants, and that includes the seeds. Obviously when a colony becomes very small it needs all the seed each plant produces, in order to maintain its own numbers. As a general rule, you should not collect your propagation material from plants which are growing on their own. Try and find a big, healthy colony of the wildflower or shrub, and collect seed or cuttings from there. That way you will do no harm. Collect the smallest amount of seed you can, and once you have taken seed from the wild, do make sure you use it. It is a terrible waste to pick seed and then leave it unsown.

As wildlife gardens become more popular, there will be less and less need to collect seed and cuttings from the wild. Wildlife gardeners will be able to exchange seed, and whole plants for that matter, and when we reach that stage, those wildflowers will definitely be safe from extinction.

When it comes to collecting, do avoid raiding the very special habitats. You don't need to plant rare wildflowers at all. There are some very common ones which make wonderfully colourful border flowers – yellow toadflax, purple toadflax, knapweed, hawkweed, oxeye daisy. A lot of these you can find growing on urban wasteland. I have collected most of the wild seed for my flower-garden from plants growing in the brick rubble of a demolition site less than a quarter of a mile from Birmingham Town Hall.

You do need to go to the appropriate wild habitat in order to collect seed of the more specialised wildflowers, of course. Again, you should avoid nature reserves at all costs, and don't take from very small pockets of habitat, either. Most of my wetland species have been grown from seed collected along a very weedy stretch of derelict canal in the Black Country. Flag iris, flowering rush, burr-reed, water plantain, lesser spearwort and watermint all grow there in abundance, and the seedheads are easy to get at. The greater spearwort and ragged robin came from a patch of canal-side marshland which was unfortunately being tipped on, and I think that is perhaps the one time when it is permissible to dig up a whole plant. You must get permission from the owners first, though, and you should also contact your County Naturalists Trust, to tell them what you plan to do.

If the plants are about to be destroyed completely, then it seems silly not to transplant them, but do make sure there is nothing you can do to stop the development first. The best place for wild plants to grow is the place where they have always grown. Your garden can only ever be second best.

If it is seed of meadow plants you need, see if you can find a local road verge that has plenty of wildflowers. Now that Highway Authorities have begun economising by mowing the grass less often, some of the green reservations and embankments have really begun to blossom. On the deeper soils you will tend to find fairly vigorous wildflowers such as teasels, cow parsley and thistle, but on the poorer thinner soils, there is often a whole kaleidoscope of colourful meadow flowers. On one patch of steep embankment half a mile from here I have collected seed of oxeye daisy, knapweed, yellow rattle, lady's bedstraw, yarrow, purple vetch, field scabious, wild carrot, meadow buttercup and birdsfoot trefoil, as well as several of the prettier dwarf grasses. This little roadside community must have arrived as seed in a lorry-load of soil when the road was first built, and despite my selective harvesting, the spread of wildflowers grows bigger every year.

Another obvious place to collect meadow-flower seed ought to be the local park. If the green revolution really takes off, and park-keepers begin to manage their green deserts as meadows once again, I can imagine great summer seed-gathering parties, with lots of eager wildlife gardeners harvesting a couple of cowslip seedheads here, or a fritillary seed there. For the time being, though, we must restrict our seed gathering to the more common wildflowers, on those accessible bits of grassland that have somehow escaped the mower and the herbicide.

Woodland wildflowers are rather more difficult. Flowery woodlands are now sadly few and far between, and they all very obviously belong to somebody. It isn't really advisable simply to crash into the nearest wood and start snipping away at the bluebell seed pods. I suggest that first of all you contact both the local Parks Department and the County Naturalists Trust, and ask them if they manage any woodlands where you might be allowed to collect a little seed. Look out, too, for rich old hedgerows. You may not find primroses or wood anemones there, but you can often find the less choosy species such as campion, bluebell and foxglove, and you will be able to tell quite easily whether or not the hedgerow community can stand the loss of a few dozen seeds.

You can grow trees and shrubs from seed, too. Although it may seem easier and quicker to root a cutting, seed propagation is better really, because it gives you a bit of variety amongst the resulting plants, and that makes your habitat look more natural. You may be tempted to take cuttings from a hawthorn bush because it has a particularly heavy crop of fruit each year, or you like the pink tint in its May blossom – but if you take cuttings, every one of the resulting plants will be identical, and you will lose the interest that seedling variation brings.

The general rule with the seed of most species seems to be to collect it when it has just reached ripeness, and sow it straight away. Certainly that is the case with acorns, for example, and it seems to help with the germination of quite a number of notoriously difficult wildflowers.

Where the seed is enclosed in a fleshy fruit, the presence of the flesh seems to build up an inhibiting factor in the seed it contains, and for quite a number that inbuilt resistance to germination is 'unlocked' when the fruit is digested by a bird or a mammal, and the stripped seed is then excreted. Hawthorn, for example, is a very difficult seed to germinate until it has been part-digested by a bird. If you are propagating from fleshy fruit – and the common examples would be bramble, elderberry, rosehip, hawthorn, sloe, honeysuckle and guelder rose – extract the seed from the fruit pulp as soon as you can. For a small number of seedlings you can do that quite easily by squeezing the individual fruit until the seeds pop out. For larger quantities you can use a food-blender to chop up the fruit, in which case most of the tough little seeds will survive. Alternatively the juicier, edible fruits can be used to make wine or jelly, and the seed can then be extracted by drying the resulting pulp. I can't think of a better excuse for making elderberry or blackberry wine. No one will believe you simply did it for the seeds!

A great many seeds do incorporate a delaying mechanism which can stop them germinating for several years in some cases. Sometimes this inhibition is caused by chemicals, as seems to be the case with the pulp-fruit seeds, and sometimes there is simply a tough coating around the seeds, which has to be penetrated by moisture before germination can take place. If the seed looks tough, or if you have experienced difficulty in the past, it is well worth encouraging more rapid germination by using various techniques known collectively as stratifying.

The easiest method of all I described earlier in the book. Simply sow the seed in sandy soil in a pot or box. Put this outside in a cold, exposed position and let the worst of the icy winter weather break down the barriers. As an alternative, you can try physically damaging the seed's thick outer coating. Rub the seed between sheets of sandpaper, so that the shiny surface is scratched. Alternatively, for very big seeds such as some of the vetches, for example, you can nick each seed with a penknife, or scrape away a groove with a nailfile. A dilute acid is a useful way of breaking the inhibition, though you have to be careful not to overdo it. Dilute sulphuric acid is the usual choice, and a fairly brisk rinse is often all that is needed. There are one or two species that need high temperatures rather than low ones to help them germinate. These are the plants that often seem to colonise burnt areas. Gorse is a good example, and its shiny pealike seeds are notoriously difficult to germinate. The secret is to put the seed in a twist of newspaper, and then set fire to it. Foresters use the same technique for preparing the seed of lodgepole pine (*Pinus contorta*), a North American pioneer of ground cleared by forest fires.

Sowing and growing-on is just the same for wild plants as for anything else. In order to germinate, the seed needs adequate air, moisture and warmth. A sandy compost, shallow sowing and light watering from below satisfy that requirement. Once germination has taken place, high humidity is important, to stop the delicate little seedlings drying out. A polythene bag supported as a mini-greenhouse over the top of the pot of seedlings is usually all that is needed, and plenty of light is essential if the seedlings are not to grow straggly and weak. Woodland species will benefit from a bit less light than meadow and wasteland species. Wetland wildflowers will obviously need much more water, and a little leaf-mould seems to help with woodland species, too. Patience is a very important ingredient in all of this. It may be several seasons before some of the seed germinates. Don't throw the pots away in disgust.

You may decide to propagate one or two plants vegetatively. Perhaps you have found a particularly sweet and juicy crop of blackberries, and you don't want to run the risk of producing a tasteless, seedy offspring from seed. Perhaps you only want one or two plants and simply don't fancy the fiddling about with seed propagation.

Most of the shrubs and trees are best grown from softwood cuttings. Wait until mid-June, choose a vigorous, non-flowering side shoot, peel it off the main stem, take off the lower leaves, and stick it peeled end down into the side of a pot of gritty soil. Put a polybag over the top to keep the air humid, and stand the pot in a saucer so you can keep the compost moist, but not wet. The cutting should produce roots within a week or two, and once it shows signs of growing, pot it on, or plant it out.

For climbers and more straggly shrubs, you might like to try layering. This time, instead of taking the cutting off the parent plant, bend a healthy growing stem right over, anchor the tip of the shoot to the soil, and leave it there until it roots. Once the tip begins to produce a new plantlet you can cut through the old stem and transplant the new offspring. This is a very good way of propagating honeysuckle, old man's beard, wild rose and blackberry.

Once you have clumps of wildflowers established in your wildlife garden, you can help them to multiply quickly by digging them up, dividing them and replanting the plantlets. The procedure is described clearly in every book about herbaceous borders. Some clumps will be easy to split. Primroses can be teased into smaller plants with fingers and thumbs, and the waterside plants tend to be very easy to split. For the bigger, toughest clumps, lift them in late summer or early spring, and force the whole mass of roots apart by using a couple of garden forks. So long as you replant immediately, the divided clumps will benefit very much from being split up and spread out every few years.

If your habitats are working, once the various appropriate wildflowers are established, you will probably find your garden is generating a mass of seedlings for other people to use. In only its second season I was able to collect dozens of seedlings from my woodland edge and my marsh habitat. Once you begin to recognise the leaf-shape of seedlings such as meadowsweet, ragged robin, pink campion and violet, you will be able to make good use of them, instead of simply pulling them out as weeds. Perhaps one of the most useful things you could do for nature conservation, is to pot up a range of your garden-grown wildflower seedlings each year, and offer them to your local County Trust. They will be able to sell them to other would-be wildlife gardeners, and your efforts will kill three birds with one stone. You will avoid being overrun, the wildflowers will be established in yet another safe patch of garden and the Trust will raise some cash to help with other important aspects of nature conservation.

Chapter 12

A rich tapestry of wildlife

SO FAR I have tended to talk about the wild plants and animals as if they are locked into one habitat or another. In fact, so far as the animals in your wildlife garden are concerned, the interchange *between* habitats is critical too. Build your pond in the centre of a sea of tarmac, and the variety of wildlife it could support would be extremely limited. The snails would be OK, and one or two of the long-distance flying insects would make it backwards and forwards across the wasteland, but the frogs and the newts, the toads and the less adventurous migratory insects would be lost. They need much more than the pond itself if they are to survive and complete their life-cycles.

In the short term you may be able to rely on borrowing wildlife from outside your garden, but it is important to work towards providing a variety of habitats of your own, which will complement one another.

Watch your resident robin for a few minutes. He will spend most of his time in the woodland-edge or the hedgerow, with his chestnut-brown back camouflaging him against the leaf-shade. His song will tell you where to look. The minute you appear with your garden fork he will be down at your feet, head cocked on one side, waiting to pounce on anything that wriggles as you begin to dig. Watch for a little while, and sooner or later you will see him flutter over to the pond for a drink, or nip across to the compost heap for a quick dig around after mini-beasts. When it comes to the breeding season the robin will patrol his territory aggressively, singing at the top of his voice, and again the woodland-edge will provide a useful song-perch, but for nest-sites the robin needs dense undergrowth and the hedge bottom becomes important. Generally speaking, a pair of robins will occupy about an acre of suburban gardens, but without the range of habitats I have just described, they may need to push out the boundaries, and you might have to share your robins with dozens of your neighbours.

This newt hatched out in my garden pond, but in late summer it migrated through the long grass of the meadow, and spent the autumn days and all the winter in damp cool beneath a rotting log.

You may well be lucky enough to have a greater-spotted woodpecker visiting your bird feeding station, but remember it needs a big tree with dead branches somewhere close by if it is to nest successfully.

By contrast the wren and the dunnock are far less adventurous, and seem hardly ever to stray from the hedge-bottom and the woodland-edge. Blackbirds are woodland birds, and certainly they spend a great deal of time scratching around amongst the leaf litter of the woodland-edge, but they also like to feed on the lawn area. I watch them pacing attentively from one spot to the next listening intently, and then stabbing with their beaks and dragging out another poor unsuspecting earthworm. The songthrush hunts for snails amongst the ivy and the woodland-edge undergrowth, but usually brings them out into the sunshine to smash the shell on her anvil. In the nesting season the pond becomes a crucial part of her total environment, since songthrushes line their nests with mud.

Some of the big dragonflies that visit the pond to breed and lay their eggs travel around a good deal. The hawkers are probably the most spectacular, and they eat hundreds of small insects every day. Although the nymph spends all of its two or three years in the water, munching its way through tadpoles all spring and summer, the adult hunts mainly along the woodland-edge and the more overgrown hedgerows. In fact, it is presumably this widespread hunting which brings hawkers into contact with new ponds so quickly. Even when they are jerking around a foot or two above my pond, they constantly sweep off over the meadow to snatch up a fly or midge that catches their eye. I have even seen the brown hawker catch a cabbage-white butterfly on the wing, and then retire to a twig of the nearby apple tree, nip off the white wings which flutter to the ground, and then chew its way through the body.

The actual amount of wildlife in our relatively new garden really has amazed me. My notebook confirms it, of course, but just a casual glance out of the window at any time of the year leaves me in no doubt that the garden is full of life. Obviously, it is the big creatures that you notice first, and one of the biggest we have seen so far is the muntjac deer. This is tiny by deer standards, in fact much the same size as a fox, but it really is a bit of a shock to glance out and see a beautiful wild creature wandering nervously along the 'woodland-edge'. In fact, muntjac are becoming quite common in the suburbs of southern Britain. They were originally imported from China to Woburn in 1900, but inevitably a few escaped and they have gradually spread. They are very secretive as a rule, but you may well have seen one in the car headlights and taken it for a fox which had lost its tail. Our visitor only stayed long enough to eat the flowers off every one of my precious clumps of bluebells, and then left. Another favourite food, particularly in winter, is the succulent little red shoots on rose bushes. I aready knew there was a muntjac about because a local gardener had very thoughtfully brought me a jam jar full of 'strange droppings' to identify. The last thing I want to do is solicit parcels of droppings from all over the place, but it is quite often the only evidence you have that some unusual creature has passed through your garden,

Urban foxes have become very common in recent years. They hunt by night, and do a good deal of scavenging around dustbins and birdtables too. Look out for their tracks in the winter snow, and listen for the blood-curdling scream of the vixen in the mating season. Foxes spend the daylight hours lying low under garden sheds, on garage roofs, and even up trees.

and on this occasion I was able to impress my enquirer with a rapid identification. Believe it not, there is an excellent book on the subject, and although muntjac itself is not included, the droppings are just like a smaller version of those produced by fallow deer. You might not think that something as big as a muntjac could possibly pass unnoticed through your neighbourhood, but this is where the wildlife corridors are so important. This little deer generally clings to the overgrown areas and presumably finds no difficulty travelling undetected along railway cuttings, canal embankments and old hedgelines.

Muntjac make quite a noise when they are disturbed – a sort of short, sharp bark – and their alternative name is barking deer.

With quite a few of your wild visitors it may be the sound, rather than the sight, that gives them away. Certainly that is the way I discovered that we had a visiting lesser spotted woodpecker, for instance. It has a high-pitched piping call which is quite unmistakable once you know it. The foxes give themselves away by calling too. The blood-curdling scream of a vixen is unforgettable, and again these marvellous mammals are experts at passing through suburbia unnoticed. Unlike the muntjac, foxes are mainly nocturnal, and escape a lot of human attention by operating after dark, but in hard winters particularly, or when they have cubs to feed, they can often be seen loping home with a guilty look after a hard night of scavenging. Urban foxes are extremely inventive so far as daytime hideaways are concerned. They lie up on shed roofs, in drain culverts and under brambles. The prize for artistic presentation, though, must surely go to the wily old dog-fox who sleeps all day stretched lazily across a raft of clematis montana in the garden of a friend of mine. The clematis has grown up and over an old hawthorn tree, and produced a solid tangle of twisted stems. The fox has no difficulty in climbing the tree, and is quite invisible from below, though you do get a lovely view of him, with his orange coat contrasting beautifully with the pink of the flowers, if you look down from a bedroom window.

If you don't see or hear your foxy visitors, you may well smell them. Foxes mark their territory with a powerful, musky scent, and if you have a marking post in your garden you will certainly know about it.

There are a number of other British predatory mammals that inhabit wildlife gardens. I have devoted a good deal of space to the hedgehog already, and this endearing, bumbling little creature does find his way into some very urban gardens. Hedgehogs are extremely agile climbers, and seem quite capable of scaling high brick walls with scarcely a pause for breath. They clamber up like a giant clockwork toy, roll up for protection and then drop softly down on the other side. They also have an amazing ability to squeeze through small holes. If your garden wall or fence looks to be too much of a challenge for a mountaineering hedgehog to tackle, try cutting a small hole, say 100mm square, at ground level: it will become quite a thoroughfare for small creatures and will save your hedgehog a bit of time.

Badgers are still pretty rare in gardens. They do need quite extensive territory, and not many gardens are big enough to cope with the upheaval of an expansive badger sett. They do have a number of smaller predatory relatives though, and some of these may well turn up from time to time. The weasel is tiny – about 200mm from nose to tail – and very inquisitive. It streaks across open spaces, very close to the ground, and will occasionally stop, sit up on its haunches and inspect you. The stoat is rather bigger – perhaps 350mm long – and it moves quite differently, with a bounding gait. It tends to be less active during daylight, too. Both are very vicious little carnivores, hunting along the hedge bottom and over the stone bank for voles and mice, and weasels are quite capable of climbing up trees and entering nestboxes to catch the young birds. In hard weather you may even see them scramble up and take food from the birdtable. These fascinating animals need plenty of cover, and very definitely travel along hedgerows and other ecological corridors.

Squirrels are the other large mammals you are likely to have visit you. Although they are always shown in cuddly pose, gnawing away at hazelnuts, they do actually eat quite a wide range of things. Most of us are never likely to see red squirrels, of course, because they are now confined to a few very localised colonies, but grey squirrels are becoming more and more common, and they can do a great deal of damage to young trees. They seem particularly fond of the green shoots of sycamore. In our garden they occasionally turn up to pick over the strawberries, and they have become very expert at breaking into the bags of peanuts hanging from the birdtable. They can be a real problem in spring, too, when they sometimes turn their attention to young birds in their nests, and they will also take eggs. Generally speaking, they will use your garden only in its service-station capacity, and build their tree-top drey or nest-bundle in a clump of trees where there is rather more space.

The more mobile a species is, the more chance you have of enjoying a visit. It isn't just animals that move around, of course, and perhaps the most extensive of travellers are the fungi. They colonise by producing thousands of tiny spores which are easily transported in the air, and form part of the aerial plankton, along with pollen grains and a few species of very small animals. Fungi are saprophytes, and live by digesting dead material. Your wildlife garden will contain a good deal of dead vegetable matter, from logs to lettuce leaves, and whilst many of the fungi are very specific, their spores are so numerous that if you provide a suitable habitat you are likely to be colonised. Certainly you can expect some spectacular toadstools on your logs in autumn, and if you have used chopped bark or shredded wood as a mulch you can expect to see crowds of colourful toadstools popping up all over the place. You may be lucky,

There is a lot of wasteland in towns. You may well be borrowing your service station garden wildlife from a spot like this. Make sure it isn't under threat.

and have a delicious species like chanterelle growing under the birch trees of your woodland-edge, but for the most part they are likely to be better for looking at than eating. Many of the most spectacular toadstools belong to fungi that only seem to thrive in ancient habitats, but one or two of the rarest are actually fungi of new landscapes. There are quarries, for instance, with brand new landscapes sporting extremely unusual species, and on a large brick-strewn National Car Park site in the centre of Birmingham a rare 'morel' suddenly appeared a year or two ago, much to the surprise of the man on the gate. He wasn't used to queues of bobble-hatted botanists actually paying to visit his car park and photograph bits of it.

Some of the flowering plants are surprisingly mobile, too. There are quite a number which spread by producing seeds with wings or parachutes, and they can blow in, but they mostly have very tiny seed

Everyone loves hedgehogs, but they need much more than the occasional saucer of bread and milk if they are to survive. They eat slugs galore each summer, and can suffer from a buildup of poison in modern gardens. They also need a safe, undisturbed pile of dead leaves for hibernation.

with relatively little in the way of an energy store, and they need open, cultivated soil if they are to colonise. Plants like sow thistle (*Sonchus* spp), hawkweed (*Hieracium umbellatum*), groundsel (*Senecio vulgaris*) and willowherb (*Epilobium* spp) will certainly keep up a constant bombardment, but will only actually establish themselves in the vegetable patch or other patches of loose soil. Some other species may simply appear once the habitat is right. I have hedge mustard in my garden which now fills the woodland-edge habitat with handsome white flowers, and white deadnettle, too. Both these plants I suspect were always around, but my change of circumstances has suited them both particularly well and they have thrived.

Other species must be brought in by birds and animals. Goose grass (*Galium aparine*) or cleavers is a good example of a plant whose seeds cling to the fur of passing foxes and dogs. Burdock (*Arctium lappa*) travels the same way, though here it is a whole fruit containing several big black seeds which is transported. A burdock plant has sprung up in my garden, and I am quite happy as it is excellent for butterflies in August, and then attracts flocks of seed-eating birds in the autumn and winter. Birds act as agents for introducing a good many new plants into the garden, too. Plant birch or alder through a mulch of chopped bark, and fairly soon you will begin to see seedlings of hawthorn, bramble and dogrose popping up. You will probably find seedlings of garden shrubs such as mahonia, berberis and cotoneaster, too. This is the result of birds roosting in your saplings having gorged themselves on berries from elsewhere. The seed passes through the bird unharmed, and you finish up with a new seedling. You may find oak trees springing up if there are large oaks in the neighbourhood. These are clear evidence that you have a jay active in your garden, picking acorns and carrying them off to be buried in your woodland-edge. Squirrels also bury hazelnuts, and I remember being thrilled one year to discover hazel seedlings appearing all over the far end of the garden. I thought at first that this was the work of an absent-minded hoarding squirrel, but then remembered that for a week or two after Christmas two years before, I had used a bowl of hazelnuts as ammunition for throwing at the local cats. These little seedlings had come back to haunt me.

As your wildlife garden develops, I promise you will see far more birds, you will hear far more scuffles and squeaks from small mammals if you venture out after dark, and you will even look on new types of weeds as 'firsts' for the species list. The really astounding success of wildlife gardening, though, is at the creepy-crawly end of the business. The increase in the variety and number of insects, spiders and other invertebrates is quite astonishing. Every time I walk through my garden I discover another little creature I have never seen before. My hazel has wonderful shiny shieldbugs on it, the birch leaves are decorated in midsummer with the lively larvae of the birch sawfly, each one of which springs to attention by standing on its head as you approach. Lift a log and there is a mass of spectacular beetles and other fast-moving mini-beasts scattering for cover. If I sit and watch a patch of marigolds for a minute or two, numerous different species of bees, wasps and wasp look-alikes will visit. Peer down among the grasses of the meadow, and there are spiders galore, some of them beautifully camouflaged to blend in among the green and gold of the mini-jungle. Many of these mini-beasts are very cleverly disguised, and you need to spend time sitting and concentrating on a small patch of the garden before you really notice them. There are crab-spiders that change colour to suit their setting, and sit amongst the creamy flowers of the cowparsley tribe, legs outstretched, almost invisible and ready to pounce. Many of the caterpillars are subtly marked, and disappear into their habitat. Some of the moth caterpillars look exactly like snapped-off twigs, and stand motionless if you approach them. Others, like the poplar hawkmoth and the orange-tip caterpillars are just the same green as their food plants, and blend in perfectly. There are others, of course, which adopt quite the opposite strategy and stand out like sore thumbs. These gaudy little creatures are

Your garden is just the beginning. Here is a typical town park – imagine how marvellous it could be if we began wildlife gardening on a grand scale.

usually poisonous or unpalatable, and their markings warn off the wisest of the local birds.

All of these wild plants and animals depend on one another for survival. The blackbird that helps to establish the new bramble seedling may well be back a couple of years later to collect its fruity reward, or it may visit the first spring after transplanting, to pick off caterpillars to feed to its young. The fungi that have their spores spread by browsing slugs are at the same time helping break down the dead wood to a state where the slugs themselves can feed on it. They in turn provide food for the hedgehogs which perhaps hibernated there when the logs were less rotten.

Remember that native plants and rotting vegetable matter are the basic materials of wildlife gardening. Place them in their appropriate habitat setting, and then watch carefully. The animal life will move in and colonise the habitat, and as the garden matures your resident web of native wildlife will become more and more intertwined, and will provide you with more and more enjoyment from your wildlife garden.

Chapter 13

Study wildlife

THE LAST thing I want to do is to make people take their garden wildlife terribly seriously. The wildlife in my own garden is an immense source of *pleasure* to me. I enjoy the company of songbirds, and the spectacle of dragonflies. It also gives me a great deal of satisfaction to know that I am, genuinely, making a difference to the survival chances of a whole range of wild plants and animals.

If you do want to use your garden for more serious study, though, there is a great need to learn more about the habits and characteristics of even our most familiar wildlife. You will get an extra level of enjoyment out of learning some of the secrets of your resident plants and animals, and you may well discover something which even the most learned of experts have overlooked. You can begin modestly enough by doing no more than keeping a diary. Having changed your garden, or created a whole set of brand new wildlife habitats, you should find it interesting simply to keep a record of the way the wildlife community develops. If you are a methodical, precise sort of person, you may want to measure the growth of your trees, or the spread of your original clumps of wildflowers, and you may want to combine your wildlife observations with a detailed record of the weather. I'm afraid my records don't stretch that far, but I am very interested in building up a picture of the rate of colonisation, and noting population changes. All I do is to spend as much time as I can sitting quietly in the garden, or moving slowly around the paths – looking. Each time I spot something new, I make an entry in my notebook – nothing elaborate, you understand, just time, date and what it is I have spotted. Of course, some of the things I've noticed for the first time could well have been around for ages, but there is a general picture building up on the way the diversity of wildlife is increasing as each habitat becomes more mature.

This simple diary already makes fascinating reading – for me at least.

It jogs my memory about all sorts of exciting discoveries I have made, and the act of writing up each observation is useful too, in that it forces me to check the names of things, and I learn a lot that way. The pond has provided the most constant stream of 'new entries' in the first couple of years, with whirlygig beetles and pondskaters arriving almost instantly, and great diving beetles turning up in great numbers in the second summer. I've noted more and more birds using the pond for both drinking and bathing, with much more of the splashing taking place in the cold of the winter than in the warmth of summer. The meadow has a lengthy list of resident plants, with the seeded area producing many of its prettiest flowers in the second, rather than the first season. The meadow's insect life has developed almost as dramatically as the pond's although I must admit that I find it much more difficult to identify meadow creepy-crawlies – there are just so many different kinds of beetles, spiders and 'little black flies'.

The list of garden birds grows longer all the time, with most of the later additions visiting the woodland-edge. I think the lesser spotted wood-pecker is probably the most exciting so far, though I must admit I smiled a little the day I was able to add a very noisy, cream coloured parakeet to the list. My garden is just two years old now. It is about a quarter of an acre in area, and so far we have had forty different species of bird visiting us. The list of breeding birds is much shorter, of course, but even that is quite pleasing. Robins have nested in both years. Wrens have bred, as have bluetits, great-tits, songthrushes, blackbirds and greenfinches.

Of course these simple observations teach you things which help you improve your wildlife garden. You will quickly learn that the small birds are unlikely to use a nestbox that is exposed to full sun. They seem to know that a shady box is less likely to stifle the fledglings later in the spring. I am particularly interested in insects, and my notes about the flowers that insects feed on are helping me to improve the nectar service station year by year. That perhaps is the next thing I should suggest. Once you have settled into the habit of recording things you notice, why not make a special study of one particular aspect of the wildlife you observe? Here the choice is endless. Just choose a subject that seems to be throwing up some interesting, general observations, and begin to keep more detailed records. The dragonflies on my pond are a case in point. The first year, I was more than satisfied simply spotting each new species as it turned up, making a note of its antics, and using a reference book to sort out which species was which. I learned, for instance, that the broad-bodied blue darter arrived very early in the summer, and had disappeared by mid-July. By contrast the enormous common brown hawkers visited the pond regularly until well into September, and the common sympetrum seemed to come and go for short spells all through the summer.

As the second summer went by, I began to take more of an interest in the different ways in which the various species of dragonflies mate, and more particularly the quite varied and apparently very specific sites they choose for egg-laying. The hawkers seem to prefer to lay their eggs on the damp logs of my marsh-side causeway, whilst the golden female of the blue darter bobs along, placing her eggs individually on plants just below the water-surface. The sympetrum does likewise, but with this species, the male and female bob along in tandem. Next summer I intend studying the various breeding performances in much more precise detail.

I mentioned food preferences for garden butterflies in Chapter 8. Birds are even easier to observe, and you can carry out a very interesting study by watching your birdtable closely. Note which are the first birds to land after you put the food out. Which are the most aggressive birds, and do the same ones always dominate the pecking order? Do any of the species prefer to feed on the ground? Is there a pattern to the number of times any particular bird looks up in between pecks? Which birds carry their food away from the table to eat it? I am quite certain that as you watch the birds, you will notice other aspects of the birdtable activity that you will want to know more about, and you can simply start another set of detailed records.

One of the nice things about noting down your wildlife observations is that you can begin to discover patterns of behaviour, and to predict when certain things will happen. If you do keep a note of weather conditions, for instance, then you may be able to tell when you can expect your first visit from winter migrants such as redwings and fieldfares. They usually turn up the day after heavy snow falls and gales in the North Sea. If you hear the announcement on the shipping forecast, you can have a pile of apples on the lawn to greet them, and increase your chances of a visit even more.

Your records will tell you where the various birds nest, and it is interesting to build up a picture of when they begin to nest each year, too. Some species will start very early, as early as February some years, but others don't even arrive here for the summer until May. Most species are very choosy about nest sites. I have already suggested that sunny nestboxes are unpopular, and you will remember that the height of nesting varies from species to species, too. You might like to run a simple experiment to see what building materials each bird prefers. You can do this by analysing the old nests, of course, by pulling them to bits to see what they are made of. I have great fun each year hanging a bag of various suitable nesting materials, and watching the birds flying in to collect them. Some species are perfectly happy pulling their lengths of wool, old oak leaves or feathers from a net hanging in the apple tree. Others simply won't use that source at all, but are prepared to tug away at the goodies if they are put in a similar net, but anchored to the ground. The songthrush and the housemartins both use mud in their building, and the edge of the pond is a useful source of suitable sticky stuff for both of them.

Most breeding birds are extremely territorial, and when the season begins, you will notice that birds which tolerated one another quite happily in the struggle of winter suddenly become very aggressive indeed. It is interesting to work out a map of territories for your garden and the area around it. The best way to begin this study is to get up very, very early on a couple of mornings, after you know the nesting season has begun. If you can manage to be out in the garden about an hour before dawn – and in late April that probably means before 4 a.m. – then you should have the mind-blowing experience of hearing the dawn chorus from the very beginning. Just close your eyes, and count on your fingers as you hear each new voice join in the chorus. You will soon run out of fingers, and I promise you that even in the depths of the city you will be amazed by the volume, and the beauty of the sounds. If you have a portable tape-recorder, it is worth taping your dawn chorus, so that you can listen to it at a more civilised hour, and try to work out who all the performers are. For the territory project, though, you need to listen carefully and make a note whenever you hear the same birdsong coming from two or more places. The dawn chorus isn't a great, happy choir of chummy feathered friends, all showing how glad they are to be alive. It is actually a battle in sound. Each male bird is sitting firmly in his nesting territory, and shouting for all he is worth that this is his patch! Woe betide any other breeding male of the same species who dares to try to move in. When you hear two different great-tits piping away, each one is telling the other to stick to his own territory, and that helps you to work out just how many breeding pairs, how many territories there are around your garden. Last spring I had the pleasure of hearing stereo song-thrushes. The two cock thrushes would sit each morning and evening on the topmost branch of their respective pear trees, one in the garden next door and the other two doors away on the other side. They sang away at one another, with me marvelling at the liquid sounds as I crouched sleepily in the middle. The thing that I found particularly interesting was that my garden pond appeared to be in a sort of no-man's land right on the boundary of the two territories. Having shown one another who was boss on each side of the garden, the birds could then be seen meeting at the waterhole, collecting a beakful of mud and wet leaves each, and then flying off in opposite directions to carry on with the construction work.

Most of the time there is no obvious boundary line on the ground, but just some invisible zone that both birds recognise. Sometimes, though, you can see that a boundary is formed by a hedge or a building. In the same season that I had two pairs of songthrushes divided by my wildlife garden, I had three pairs of bluetits all nesting within the garden. Each pair occupied a different nestbox, but the house provided a very solid

lump in the middle which conveniently kept the territorial birds apart. There was one pair on each side of the house, and the third was right down at the opposite end of the garden, nesting in a box on the fence. It was listening that led me to discover the wren nesting in a hole under the eaves of my office, and this noisy little bird leaves you in no doubt about its territorial rights. I also discovered a robin nesting in a nestbox with an oversized hole at the far end of the garden, by sitting and listening carefully. If you want to see a dramatic demonstration of territorial behaviour, try intruding into the local robin's stamping ground. Stick up a dummy robin – a brown mitten with a piece of red cloth fixed to the front will do – and within minutes the resident cock robin will be beating the stuffing out of the impostor. Do take the dummy away once you have seen the performance, though, otherwise the real robin could become quite distressed.

Having observed how possessive nesting birds are, you can probably realise that the birdtable could be a bit of a handicap. If there are lots of different birds flying in for their daily snack, this will upset the birds nesting close by, and they are quite likely to move out. Stop feeding when birds start to take an interest in nearby nestboxes or, if the garden is big enough, keep the boxes at least 20 metres away from the birdtable.

The best guide to the health of a habitat lies in the happiness of its creepy-crawlies. You will see lots of them around in the garden, of course. Turn over a log, the centipedes wriggle away, and the woodlice rush around in all directions desperately trying to get out of the limelight. Dozens of little black hunting spiders decorate the sunny surface of the shrub border in midsummer, and there are holes bitten out of almost every leaf in the wildlife garden. If you want more than just a passing acquaintance with your mini-beasts, it is quite easy to trap them. Concentrate particularly on the ones that roam around at ground level at first. If you can build up a picture of the variety and number of creatures living in different parts of your garden, it will give you a clearer idea of how well your various habitats are working. All you need is a set of miniature mammoth traps. Most of the beetles, millipedes and other crawling creatures move around without much concern for the road ahead. If you put a hole in their path, then the odds are they will fall in. You can come along later and see what you have caught. Choose a number of different habitats around the wildlife garden – the close-mown lawn, a patch of rough meadow, the vegetable garden, somewhere in the woodland-edge – select as many different types of mini-environment as you can. Then dig a hole in each location just the right size to take a smooth-sided plastic cup. Drop a cup into each hole, put something juicy and delicious in the bottom of each to act as bait (an old, green piece of liver is irresistible) and put a flat stone over the top, propped on a pebble, to keep the rain out. Leave the traps no longer than twelve hours, and when you lift off the lid, you will find all kinds of little creatures have fallen in and been unable to clamber out. Trap for several days and nights and you should get a good picture of the mini-beasts there are around. You can refine the experiment by noting which animals are nocturnal, for instance, and only appear in the night-time traps. You can also see if there is a preference for different food by varying the bait. There is one great problem with pitfall trapping. The trapped mini-beasts have a tendency to eat one another. You are quite likely to have your results biased by finding one big, fat, rather smug-looking spider in the bottom of each cup, and nothing else. You can reduce the problem by inspecting the traps more frequently, before the big boys get too hungry, or you can pickle the catch immediately each creature drops in by putting a splash of formalin in the bottom of each cup. That helps to improve your scientific results, but it doesn't do a lot for the poor unfortunate wildlife. When you have finished your observations, do remember to take the cups away and fill in the hole – otherwise the mini-beast trap will carry on working until it fills up with mini-corpses.

Your pitfall-traps will almost certainly show you very clearly how much more activity there is in your wildlife garden after dark than there is in daylight. The birds and butterflies may be very active in sunshine, but most garden wildlife works on the nightshift. You really must find time to go into your garden after dark, and see what you come across. You'll be surprised how much activity there is amongst nocturnal mammals, if you have a fall of snow in the late evening. By the following morning the garden will be crisscrossed by dozens of animal tracks. Most of them will be cats, I'm afraid, but if you study them carefully, looking at the precise pattern of the pawmarks, you are quite likely to find a fox track or two. Foxes are far more common than most people realise.

You get a good idea of the amount of night-time wildlife activity there is in your garden simply by listening. Choose a warm evening, or wrap up well, and tuck yourself into the woodland-edge. Try and select a spot where the breeze is blowing off the garden and into your face. It is fairly obvious that animals which move around in the dark are likely to have particularly sensitive noses, and if the breeze is blowing from you towards them, they will smell you and know you are around much sooner. Now, just sit very quietly and listen. Nothing much will happen for a few minutes, though you may hear that fox of yours screaming somewhere in the distance, or an owl calling across the neighbourhood. As you settle in, and your eyes and ears become accustomed to the dark, you will begin to hear the garden come to life. It will start with a tiny scuffle somewhere a few feet away, but pretty soon you will have squeaks and scuffles going on all around you, and you will be amazed at the amount of secret activity there is in your mini-habitats. The night noises vary with the time of year. In spring you may be lucky enough to have the song of a nightingale for company, or at least a lovesick blackbird, kept awake by the glow of a streetlight. In late March and early April you will have the amazing racket of amorous frogs, shouting out for females to come and join them in the deep end. Late summer nights are alive with the sound of young animals. A whole family of hedgehogs may snuffle through the garden, or you may hear what sounds like dozens of mice or voles scampering around, playing amongst the dead leaves under the hedge. If there is someone in your family who is good with electronics, get a microphone rigged up in the garden, and connect it to a set of earphones in the bedroom. You can then share in all the scuffles and snuffles of the night-time garden without aggravating your arthritis or freezing to death.

If you are really brave, you can do what a friend of mine does and spend the odd night sleeping in the garden, under the stars. If you're not terribly brave, you can do what I do and sleep on a camp-bed in a sleeping bag. That way most of the creatures of the night can pass right under you, and you need never know. It must be a bit disconcerting to wake up from dreams of nightingales and moonlight to discover a hedgehog snuffling his way across your stomach.

I think the most beautiful creatures of the night are the moths. I know there are some people who hate them, but I think they are fascinating.

They have suffered from pollution and habitat destruction in recent years like everything else, but we still do have a fantastic variety of moths around, and in a good wildlife garden you can expect to find a great many different kinds. Not all of them are attracted to lights. Many of the most spectacular ones are, though, and I have seen some amazing, beautiful creatures simply by leaving on the kitchen light and popping in from time to time through the evening to check on who has turned up. I remember the swallow-tail moth. This is a beautiful, lemon yellow insect which only flies for a couple of weeks each July or August. The wing shape is very unusual, and we had three on the kitchen window in one evening. The range of moths reduces as you travel north, and my garden is at the limit of the range for quite a few species which are fairly common in the soft south. The biggest and most spectacular of these that has visited us is the red underwing. It is very big – perhaps 50mm across the wings, and it adopts the same strategy for survival as the tiger moths. Its underwings are brilliant crimson as the name suggests, and very obvious when it is flying or stretched out against the window. When threatened, though, this beautiful creature drops to the ground and closes its wings. The overwings are beautifully marked with a dusty brown and grey pattern, and the moth is perfectly camouflaged against most dark backgrounds.

There have been even bigger moths at the kitchen window from time to time. There are several species of hawkmoth which are quite common in gardens, and so far we have been visited by the poplar, the lime and the elephant hawkmoths. These are really spectacular creatures, and their caterpillars are enormous. I'm pleased to say that as far as moths are concerned the rich habitat parts of our wildlife garden work particularly well, and I have found elephant hawkmoth caterpillars feeding on the leaves of the rosebay willowherb, and the caterpillar of poplar hawk-moths munching away at the pussy-willow leaves.

You can do better than rely on chance meetings at the kitchen window. Many of the service station nectar flowers are important for night-flying moths, and a quick tour of inspection with a powerful torch on warm, overcast summer evenings will show you which are the most popular. Three of the summer flowers in my garden are streets ahead of the rest. The first is evening primrose (*Oenothera biennis*) and its big, lemon-yellow flowers are usually surrounded by moths from dusk onwards. Secondly, there are the tobacco plants (*Nicotiana affinis*). The paler ones seem best, and of course the perfume of both these lovely flowers should be a clear indication that they are likely to be good moth plants. The third winner is honeysuckle. The hawkmoths in particular seem to love it, and the long, trumpet-like flowers are perfectly suited to pollination by moths.

There is a third way of attracting night-flying moths to your service station, apart from bright lights and perfumed flowers. This is a technique know as sugaring. Moths are attracted by sweet, sugary smells. If you paint a suitably sickly-sweet mixture on a tree trunk or a fence post, then on a good evening you can be lucky and attract a whole range of night-flying insects. There are lots of 'magic' recipes, but most of them contain beer, molasses and pulped overripe fruit. I usually include a drop or two of rosewater or orange-blossom water, too. The technique seems to work particularly well on the south and east coasts of England, where migratory moths arrive exhausted and ravenous from the darkness of their cross-channel journey. Elsewhere results are usually pretty disappointing, but it is worth trying sugaring alongside a bright light. The combined pulling power may just give you a pleasant surprise.

The range of moths you are likely to find visiting your garden is enormous, and an awful lot of them look confusingly similar. If you ever get the chance, join the local experts around their mercury vapour lamp, and let them show you a few of the ones which are easy to recognise. You will be surprised how quickly you learn to identify thirty or forty of the more dramatic ones, and it will help you begin to realise how varied the different families of moths can be.

The wildlife which shares your garden can give enormous pleasure. The more carefully you study it, the more time you find to sit quietly and watch or listen, the more delighted you will be by all the evidence of the way your habitats are working. If you can take the trouble to keep notes,

As you study your wildlife garden you will notice more and more of the subtle detail. Many of the wild creatures are well camouflaged to help them survive. This is a willow beauty moth, almost invisible against the bark of a tree.

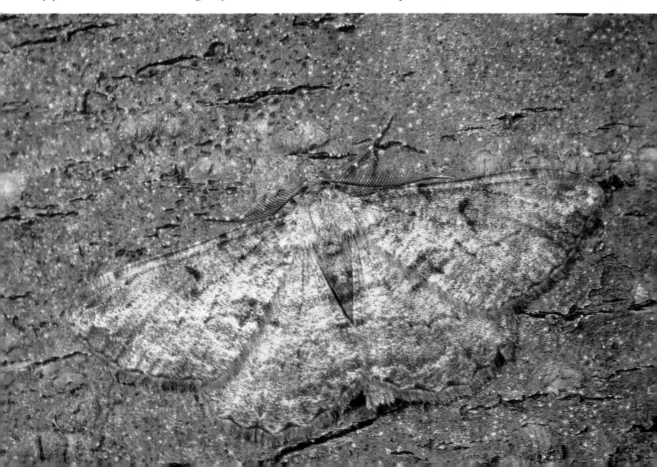

take photographs or make sketches, your knowledge will increase year by year, and as more and more people study the wildlife on their doorsteps, the detailed things we learn should help us produce more and more successful new habitats for wildlife, and understand far better the damage we can do to our environment without even knowing.

Chapter 14

Over the garden wall

AS YOUR wildlife garden gets better and better, and you learn more and more about the range of animals that use it as a service station, you will, I hope, develop a keen interest in the wildlife potential of your whole neighbourhood. I hope very much that your garden wildlife will encourage you first of all to wonder 'where it all comes from', then to play an active part in protecting the exciting wild spaces that generate your garden visitors, and finally to persuade the people who manage the 'green deserts' in your area to adopt your ideas, and create rich habitat parks, school grounds and traffic islands.

I think you will be inspired to 'sort out' the local environment, when you begin to take a real interest in the visitors to your wildlife service station. All those small tortoiseshell butterflies on the buddleia, for example: where *do* they find unsprayed nettles on which to lay their eggs? The bright yellow brimstone that is such a welcome visitor in early spring: where *did* it hibernate all winter? Is there a mass of overgrown ivy nearby and more important, where on earth will it find a bush of alder buckthorn for its caterpillars? If you don't fight to save a place for the nettles, or to stop the chopping down of the last local patch of old woodland, then the property speculators, the road (and empire) builders and your over-tidy neighbours will win, the habitat will disappear, and no matter how carefully you tend your buddleia, your garden will have fewer and fewer visiting butterflies.

One of the most useful things you can do to help your local wildlife, is to spend a few of those long, dark winter evenings studying a map of your neighbourhood. If you can get a hold of an aerial photograph, that is even better. Aim to produce a habitat plan of your area. Both the maps and the photos are expensive, but if you call in to see your local authority planning office, and explain what you are trying to do, they may well be able to let you have photocopies for a very small charge. Now – the

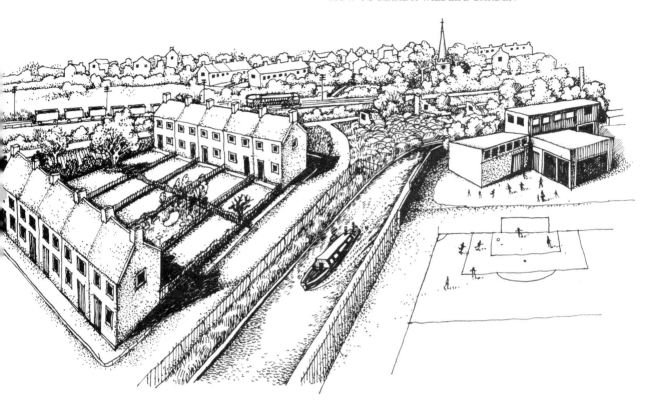

Think of your garden as a rich habitat service station in a neighbourhood wildlife network. Take a look around and you will find canals, railways and road verges acting as ecological corridors and connecting together wild green landscapes such as overgrown churchyards, railway sidings and demolition sites. Look at the official open spaces too – school playing fields and parks are often little more than green deserts but have great possibilities for habitat creation on a grand scale. Take care of your local wild areas and start to campaign for a change in the management of public open spaces. Your wildlife garden will benefit as a result.

objective is to draw up a map which tells you where your wildlife visitors are coming from. That means shading in all the green patches of land.

Some will be very easy to identify simply by looking at the map. You may have a patch of woodland or a park nearby. Others will not be quite so obvious, and this is where aerial photos can give you some real surprises. You may never have realised that the rows of grand Georgian houses round the corner are in fact enclosing a huge area of land containing big old trees, hedgerows, ponds, in fact an acre or two of 'secret' landscape that is really good for wildlife. You probably hadn't realised just how much of the old railway siding had become overgrown with bramble and silver birch woodland since the goods-yard closed twenty years ago. An aerial photo will show you these things instantly, and it will also help you pick out the wildlife corridor network. You will be able to see where an old hedge and ditch boundary survives between the individual back-to-back gardens of two adjacent housing estates. You will see how important the railway lines are, snaking through houses and factories with their ribbon of scrub and grassland habitat, and connecting the overgrown goods-yard to the school playing field.

Once you begin to build up the picture, I suggest you do a bit of footwork, and record something of the quality of the green space on your map. At its simplest level, there are basically two kinds of green landscape. There is the rough, tangled, overgrown wildscape which is so good for a whole mass of wild plants and animals, and then there is the smooth, neat, tidy, clinical green desert, which does almost nothing for nature conservation, and very little for people either. Your task is to conserve the first category and work to improve the second.

Pin up your new, unique 'neighbourhood habitat map' on the wall, and keep relating your wildlife garden to it. Each time a new species drops in, either as a casual customer or a permanent resident, have a good look at the map and try to work out where he has come from. I think I now know where my occasionally visiting lesser spotted woodpecker breeds. There are one or two big old trees with suitable dead branches in the grounds of a big house about a quarter of a mile away, and he seems to fly in from that general direction. I'm quite sure our wandering foxes have us on their route because the dustbins of the Cantonese restaurant round the corner provide such rich pickings. The aerial photo has shown me that there are several garden ponds within a few hundred metres of here, and I imagine the frogs that laid their spawn in my new pool were 'caught short' on their return journey to one or other of these. The smaller dragonflies and waterboatmen probably came from there too, though there are a couple of old mill-ponds half a mile away, and certainly that is well within the flying capability of the large hawker dragonflies and the diving beetles.

A kestrel visits my mini-meadow occasionally. There is not very much rough grassland in this bit of suburbia, but there are one or two big traffic islands, a number of overgrown allotments, and a particularly irritating patch of greenbelt farmland not far away which has been bought by a housing developer and then abandoned in the hope of changing its planning status. I imagine my kestrel hunts over all these patches of wild land, and drops into my mini-meadow now and again, once populations of voles and beetles have recovered from the last attack.

As I have said before, I don't know where my bats come from. It may be the same old trees that I think the woodpecker uses, but of course the bats arrive after dark, and so I can't really tie them down to a direction of arrival. In fact, bats seem to appear by magic. Suddenly you see one flit across a patch of open sky, and then disappear against the dark background of trees or buildings. It may be that my bats use the same roof-spaces as those visiting swifts. There are certainly a number of big Edwardian tile-hung gables to choose from close by, and they do move around of course. Pipistrelles spend quite a lot of their year roosting in individual nooks and crannies all over the place, but then all the females from quite a wide area will gather together into one hot, sunny, nursery roost, where they give birth and then each raises its own baby. They gather together again for the winter, and this time they choose a quite different spot to hibernate, preferring a roof-space or a hollow tree which is shaded and as cold as can be.

You can perhaps begin extending your circle of wildlife interest simply by thinking about the garden butterflies. As each individual appears, look up its larval food plant – a few common examples are given in the panel – and then plot the options for egg-laying on your map. There will be no end of choice for the troublesome cabbage-white – all those neat little rows of veg to choose from – but how many of them are free from pesticides? Nettles are probably in reasonable supply too, so the spring crop of small tortoiseshells and peacocks will be OK, but is there a particular patch anywhere that gets cut down in June, and then springs up again to provide the soft young shoots so necessary for the second, summer brood of caterpillars, and for the annual egg-laying of the weary migrant red admirals that arrive to breed in mid-July?

The common blue butterfly breeds in my garden, now that I have provided a few black medick plants in the meadow, but there aren't many patches of poor wasteland around here, and I think the original colonising blues probably lived as caterpillars on the leaves of a sheet of birdsfoot trefoil I have discovered decorating the abandoned coalyard of the nearby railway station. I have holly blues here, too, and they lay their autumn eggs on my ivy flowers, but I think the spring brood is raised on the flowers of a huge holly tree in the front garden of a house a few doors away. The speckled woods could well have been breeding on the couch grass in the shade of the council's shrub-beds before they discovered the few coarse grasses growing in the dappled shade of my woodland-edge habitat, but the white-letter hairstreak is not so lucky. It needs mature, healthy elm trees for its egg-laying, and since Dutch elm disease devastated this part of the country, these beautiful insects have disappeared completely from my list of garden visitors.

The butterflies are easy. They are simple to identify as adults, and their larval food plants are quite well documented. You could try the same sort of exercise with the garden birds. You know that you have far more customers at your birdtable in the winter than you could ever hope to provide nesting-sites for in your wildlife garden, so where do they all breed? Quite a few of them will stake out territories in your neighbours' gardens, of course – blackbirds in the pyracantha next door, dunnocks in the privet hedge across the road and the goldcrests have erect conifers galore to choose from. Some of the birdtable winter visitors fly miles away to breed, too. The siskins, the redwings, the bramblings and the fieldfares don't need to find a nesting-site anywhere near your garden. But what about all those greenfinches? Where is the most likely patch of bushes for them to build in? Where does the cock wren find the four or five safe holes it needs to provide an adequate choice of nests for his fickle mate to select from? If a great, ungainly grey heron flaps down to snatch a goldfish from your pond, how far has it flown from the noisy chatter of its communal heronry? Will the hollow tree used by the tawny owls last year for breeding still be there next spring, when they have need of it again?

You can have a lot of fun speculating about your wildlife garden's links with its surroundings. Draw up the ideal slug-rich circuit for your hedgehogs. Keep one ear open for reports of frogs and toads from surprised, pondless neighbours. Work out the extent of the empire ruled by the noisy magpies which build their thorny-roofed nest high in the poplar on the far side of the playing field.

A most spectacular insect passed through our garden last summer. It was a good 80mm long, and a frantic thumb through my insect book told me that it was a giant ichneumon fly (*Ryssa persuasoria*). This amazing creature has a long, sharp, thread-like spike at its back end. This is what makes it look so colossal, and it uses this ovipositor to drill down through the bark of pine trees, and lay its eggs in the larvae of the pine sawfly, known as the horntail (*Vroceras gigas*). Goodness only knows how it can tell exactly where to drill. I racked my brain to try and think of a pine plantation within range of my garden, and then realised that this spectacular visitor was, in fact, much more likely to have emerged from

CATERPILLAR PLANTS FOR GARDEN BUTTERFLIES

GRASSES

Couch (*Agropyron repens*) and **Cocksfoot** particularly in dappled shade, for the speckled wood, the ringlet and the gatekeeper.

Annual meadow grass (*Poa annua*) for the wall brown and the meadow brown.

Goat's tail grass, Soft creeping grass and **Hop-grass** for the small skipper.

Stinging nettles (*Urtica dioica*) for the red admiral, small tortoiseshell, peacock, comma and painted lady.

Black medick (*Medicago lupulina*) or birdsfoot trefoil (*Lutus corniculatus*) for the common blue, the green hairstreak and the clouded yellow.

Ivy and holly flowers for the alternative generations of the holly blue.

Sheep's sorrel (*Rumex acetosella*) or **dock** (*Rumex obtusifolius*) for the small copper.

Hedge mustard (*Sisymbrium*

officinale) for the large white, small white, green-veined white, orange-tip.

Broom (*Cytisus scoparius*) for the green hairstreak.

Lady's smock (*Cardamine pratensis*) for the orange-tip and the green-veined white.

Sweet rocket (*Hesperis matronalis*) and honesty (*Lunaria biennis*) for the orange-tip.

Nasturtium (*Tropaeolum majus*) for the large white.

Buckthorn (*Rhamnus catharticus*) for the brimstone.

Hop (*Humulus lupulus*) for the comma.

The moths are mostly just as specific in their food plant requirements as the butterfly larvae.

A good many feed on meadow grasses, and goat willow (*Salix caprea*) is particularly useful since it is suitable for some of the more spectacular garden moths' caterpillars.

the soft, pine woodwork of a new conservatory being built a few houses away. I often wonder if she ever managed to find another confused bourgeois suburban woodwasp to mate with, and where on earth she could fine a pine tree, complete with horntail larvae, in which to lay her eggs.

Once you begin to see your wildlife garden in the context of its surrounding landscape, I hope you will be galvanised into action. Perhaps you will suddenly realise what an impact the new superstore has had, in being built on the best bit of bramble-covered wasteland in the area. You might start getting angry when British Rail choose the height of the nesting season to cut down and burn all their railway embankment scrub year after year. Hopefully, you will no longer think it such a good idea for the council to spray all the nettles and long grass in the area. The untidy bits of land are the last safe sanctuary for so many of our wild plants and animals, and yet largely through ignorance, the nature-loving public press continually for neater, tidier landscapes.

If we are to cling on to our wild spaces in towns, then we have to change their image, and we need to take care of them. That task is becoming easier year by year, as word gets round that wildlife lives there. *You* can speed up the educational process through the work you do in your garden. Show people your habitat map, and choose a few simple examples to explain the corridor idea, and the need for wild places. Talk particularly to your local councillor. So often a habitat is wrecked by well-meaning decision-makers who think they are doing the best thing. If you don't bother to explain the situation, then you must share the blame for the destruction. Do show your habitat map to the officers in the local authority planning department, too. Until recently, wildlife enthusiasts were dismissed as eccentric or nutty, but planners are now beginning to incorporate ecological principles into their own plans, and they will certainly understand your mapping approach. In fact, an increasing number of local authorities now have official strategy plans for nature conservation, which are based on the kind of information *you* have to offer. Contact with the planning department has a two-way benefit. They will appreciate the detailed information you are able to provide, and in turn they will be able to keep you informed about any applications they receive which could mean destruction of important wildlife sites.

However welcoming your local planners may be, they are obviously going to prefer to deal with *representatives* of interested groups, rather than dozens of individuals, and since you are almost certainly going to have people with similar ideas to your own living close by, it is definitely worth trying to group together. There may be a suitable club or society already meeting in the area. Most of the County Naturalists Trusts now have local activity groups in each town, and you can simply feed your ideas into the nearest one. If no suitable group exists, you can start one. It is easy enough to arrange a meeting, perhaps show a few slides of local sites, put up your map, and then form a committee from the keenest of the people who turn up. You can also boost your support, and increase your chances of success considerably by encouraging the local schools to become involved. Children are the prime users of many of the wilder sites. They will often know which is the best pond for newts, or where the kestrels nest. Again there is an increasing interest in outdoor teaching of environmental education amongst the more enthusiastic teachers. You should try to see your local wildlife group as a force for education and persuasion, rather than a fighting force. Build up the information you have about the wild spaces in your area, and try to establish a regular system of consultation with the planners. I have been involved in a charitable trust called the Urban Wildlife Group since it was first formed. In just a few years we have carried out detailed surveys of a great deal of our urban open space, we have helped the local authorities prepare policy documents by providing them with detailed information, and we now visit the site of every planning application in the region, and are able to make positive comments on each, which help the decision-makers. Perhaps most important of all, we have helped make nature conservation 'respectable'. Many councillors had a sympathy for wildlife, but until we became 'organised' they seemed embarrassed to declare their interest, for fear of being labelled unrepresentative. At least they can now say that they represent *us* as well as the wildlife in their constituency.

Having an organised group of sympathisers is extremely useful when you come up against the inevitable threat to a site. The shape of our environment is determined by the amount of influence and pressure directed at the decision-making elected representatives by a whole range of lobby groups. The property speculators will be telling councillors that their new warehouse development will create jobs. The highway lobby will be stressing the immense importance of lopping a minute or two off the journey to work. The gravel extractors will be pleading that the whole economy depends on an increasing supply of cheap concrete for building. You and your friends have to join in the debate. You have to convince the politicians that woodlands tomorrow are more important than warehouses today, and it certainly helps if you can claim to represent the views of a large number of 'members'. It also helps if you can back up your understandably emotional claims with some firm, scientific evidence, collected over several years – so don't wait till there is a crisis before you form your green action group. In fact, in my experience the politicians and their advisers are generally much more impressed by the dedication and commitment of a long-established survey team than they are by the long list of obscure Latin names they are able to produce. This book is not intended as a campaign manual, but there are two tactics in particular which I find powerful in arguing for conservation of wild green space, rather than habitat destruction.

The first is the importance of wildlife, and wild spaces, to children. Even the most hardened of pro-development politicians was a child once, and all of them had a favourite wild space where they built dens, caught tadpoles and had adventures. It pays to remind them that the site under discussion is one of the few that remain, and that for the children of today and tomorrow it may offer the only chance of an escape to nature.

The second tactic arises naturally out of your survey work. Sites for development tend always to be treated in isolation. The developer or his architect will have drawn a thick black line around the site boundary, and the decision-makers may be oblivious of the way the individual site fits into its surrounding landscape. You can show that the site is, in fact, a vital link in the green network, and use your now famous map to explain how a seemingly modest little supermarket, drainage scheme or car park will effectively ruin the extended habitat and therefore the chances of survival for a whole range of attractive and popular furry and feathered friends. Hedgehogs, kingfishers, owls and butterflies are all likely to receive universal support. You need to tread warily as you enthuse about foxes, grass-snakes and dragonflies, and however fond you are of slugs and brown rats, I strongly advise you to save your enthusiasm for internal meetings only. Remember that one person's small mammal is another person's vermin.

Once you have reached the stage where the wild, unofficial spaces of the neighbourhood are being taken seriously, then you should think about turning your attention to the green deserts. There is so much potential for habitat creation in towns. There is a huge area of land committed to amenity and recreation, and there is also a vast financial commitment to planting, mowing, draining and generally manipulating the land. Despite all this commitment, the results are pitifully disappointing. Millions of trees are planted every year along the roadsides, in parks and elsewhere. An unhealthy proportion of them are exotic species, the majority of them fail to survive the first few years, and very few are planted as part of a long term woodland development programme.

Vast fleets of mowing machines tear up and down throughout the summer, scalping the urban savannah and producing a boring, uniform green grassland where nothing is encouraged to flower, and very few people would dream of walking for enjoyment. The cost of all this intensive wildlife suppression is enormous: hundreds of millions of pounds spent uncreatively year after year. If just 10% of our municipal grassland was managed more imaginatively, every town dweller could have cowslips, skylarks and meadow-brown butterflies to enjoy within a few minutes walk from home.

The way our green deserts are being managed is changing. Slowly, one or two of the more progressive parks departments are beginning cautiously to develop their parks and gardens as living landscapes suitable for wildlife *and* people. They are often discouraged, though, by the tidy-minded lobby who write and complain that the wildflower meadow experiment is simply an excuse for cutting down on mowing, or that the more naturalistic tree and shrub planting adopted as a means of initiating new woodland looks a mess in the first few seasons. It is up to you to counter those arguments. If you want a richer environment, with more birdsong and butterflies, then you have to lend your support to those park-keepers who are having a go. If you are a little hesitant, just remember that the habitat suppressors and destroyers are lobbying from a purely selfish point of view. When you shout for the rich, green, leafy alternative, you are lobbying not only for yourself, but for the children of tomorrow, and of course for the wildlife that will live in your new, improved habitats. If we all shout loudly enough, we can perhaps stop 'solving the problems of bad drainage' and enjoy the delights of wetland habitats; we can stop simply planting trees, and begin to manage new woodland. Our urban grasslands can replace the wildflower meadows we have destroyed in the countryside, and urban green space can take over from rural nature reserves as a far more extensive sanctuary for our natural heritage.

If all this talk of environmental lobbies strikes you as being a bit of a green revolution, then you are right. We simply don't have time or space left for back-tracking compromise. Remember the statistics. 97% of our meadows destroyed in 35 years. 10% of our Sites of Special Scientific Interest being ruined every single year. Spectacular species of butterflies, dragonflies, wildflowers, bats – all threatened with almost immediate extinction. Remember though, that the revolution begins with *you* in your garden.

Wildlife gardens have already saved the frog, the toad and the newt. Our bird population is enhanced dramatically by service station wildlife gardens which provide a lifeline every winter. Your garden, however small it is, can make a real difference. Boost the service station with extra pollen, nectar, seeds, water and you will help the wildlife that lives in the wild spaces beyond the garden fence. Create real habitats – a pond; a marsh; a mini-meadow; a woodland-edge – and you will have more and more wild species moving in to share your wildlife garden, to live there, breed there and survive there. Persuade your neighbours to adopt the ideas in this book, and you will soon find yourself living in a wildlife wonderland. New, exciting things will happen every day, right on your doorstep, and as your enthusiasm grows, and your circle of nature-loving friends becomes bigger and bigger, you will have no difficulty at all in finding the energy to save more and more places in your neighbourhood for you and your local wildlife to enjoy.

Useful addresses

CONSERVATION ORGANISATIONS

Amateur Entomologists' Society
355 Hounslow Road
Hanworth
Feltham
Middlesex

Botanical Society of the British Isles
c/o British Museum (Natural History)
Cromwell Road
London
SW7 5BD

01 589 6323 Ext 701

British Association of Nature Conservationists
c/o Rectory Farm
Stanton St John
Oxford
OX9 1HF

The British Butterfly Conservation Society
Tudor House
Quorn
Loughborough
Leicestershire
LE12 8AD

0509 42870

British Hedgehog Preservation Society
Knowbury House
Knowbury
Ludlow
Shropshire

British Herpetological Society
136 Estcourt Road
Woodside
London
SE25 4SA

British Trust for Ornithology (BTO)
Beech Grove
Tring

Hertfordshire
HP23 5NR

044282 3461

The Centre for Alternative Technology
Machynlleth
Powys
Wales

Common Ground
21 Ospringe Road
London
NW5

01 485 6968

The Conservation Foundation
Aviation House
129 Kingsway
London
WC2B 6NH

01 242 4637

Ecological Parks Trust
c/o The Linnean Society
Burlington House
Piccadilly
London
W1V 0LQ

01 734 5170

Fauna and Flora Preservation Society
Zoological Gardens
Regent's Park
London
NW1 4RY

01 586 0872

Field Studies Council
62 Wilson Street
London
EC2A 2BU

01 247 4651

Friends of the Earth
377 City Road

London
EC1V 1NA

01 837 0731

Garden History Society
12 Charlbury Road
Oxford

Greenpeace
36 Graham Street
London
W1 2JX

Hardy Plant Society
10 St Barnabas Road
Emmer Green
Reading
Berkshire

Henry Doubleday Research Association
Convent Lane
Bocking
Braintree
Essex

Linnean Society of London
Burlington House
Piccadilly
London
W1V 0LQ

The Mammal Society
c/o The Linnean Society
Burlington House
Piccadilly
London
W1V 0LQ

Men of the Trees
7 Abbotsfield Crescent
Tavistock
Devon
PL19 8EY

0822 3722

Nature Conservancy
Northminster House

Peterborough
PE1 1UA

0733 40345

National Council for the Conservation of Plants and Gardens
c/o RHS
Wisley
Woking
Surrey
GU23 6QB

Royal Entomological Society
41 Queens Gate
London
SW7 5HU

01 584 8361

Royal Horticultural Society
Vincent Square
London
SW1P 2PE

Royal Society for Nature Conservation
The Green
Nettleham
Lincoln
LN2 2NR

0522 752326

Royal Society for the Protection of Birds
The Lodge
Sandy
Bedfordshire
SG19 2DL

0767 80551

Rural Preservation Association
Old Police Station
Lark Lane
Liverpool 17

051 728 7011

Scottish Wildlife Trust
25 Johnstone Terrace
Edinburgh
EH1 2NH

031 226 4602

Seed Bank
44 Albion Road
Sutton
Surrey
SM2 5TF

The Tree Council
35 Belgrave Square
London
SW1X 8QN

01 235 8854

Trees for People
71 Verulum Road
St Albans
Hertfordshire
AL3 4DJ

Urban Wildlife Group
11 Albert Street
Birmingham
B4 7UA

021 236 3626

Watch
22 The Green
Nettleham
Lincoln
LN2 2NR

0522 752326

Wild Flower Society
69 Outwoods Road
Loughborough
Leics.

The Woodland Trust
Westgate
Grantham
Lincs
NG31 6LL

World Wildlife Fund-UK
Panda House
11–13 Ockford Road
Godalming
Surrey
GU7 1OU

048 68 20551

Young Ornithologists' Club
The Lodge
Sandy
Bedfordshire
SG19 2DL

Young People's Trust for Endangered Species
19 Quarry Street
Guildford
Surrey

GU1 3EH

0483 35671

SUPPLIERS OF WILDFLOWER SEED OF NATIVE ORIGIN

John Chambers
15 Westleigh Road
Barton Seagrave
Kettering
Northants
NN15 5AJ

Suffolk Herbs
Sawyers Farm
Little Cornard
Sudbury
Suffolk

Emorsgate Seeds
Middle Cottage
Emorsgate
Terrington St Clement
Kings Lynn
Norfolk

Helen McEwen
The Seed Exchange
44 Albion Road
Sutton
Surrey

W W Johnson & Sons Ltd
Boston
Lincs
PE21 8AD

NURSERIES GROWING WILDFLOWERS IN POTS

G & J E Peacock
Kingsfield Tree Nursery
Broadenham Lane
Winsham
Chard
Somerset

Davison Hardy Plants
Magnolia Cottage
North Aston
Oxford
OX5 4HU

Rural Preservation Association
Old Police Station
Lark Lane
Liverpool 17
Merseyside

Ruth Thompson
Oak Cottage Herb Farm
Nesscliff
Shrewsbury
Shropshire
SY4 1DB

WATER PLANTS

Stapeley Water Gardens Ltd
London Road
Stapeley
Nantwich
Cheshire
CW5 7JL

Acknowledgements

A great many people and experiences have inspired me to write this book.

Firstly, I must thank all those students of landscape architecture, who have taught me so much, whilst I have been trying to teach them.

Then there are all my friends, in the Urban Wildlife Group and elsewhere, who have shared with me their enthusiasm for and knowledge of Natural History.

The BBC TV Continuing Education Unit deserves my thanks, for having faith in my idea of making the film 'Bluetits and Bumblebees' when everyone else had turned it down.

Two marvellous wildlife photographers, Mike Leach and Tony Wharton have spent hours creeping up on the wildlife that inhabits my garden, and have kindly lent me one or two of their excellent slides.

I must thank Kate Hodgetts, my secretary, for painstakingly typing the manuscript, Christine Watt for checking it, and Jim Bridgen for interpreting my scribbles into such marvellous illustrations.

My wife Liz I thank for helping me in a thousand ways, and finally I owe a very special debt of gratitude to our house and garden, and to nature itself. The real inspiration behind the book, and most of the things I do, is the life I see from my window every morning.

CHRIS BAINES
Hagley

December 1984.